D1237679

Point-of-Purchase Design

WITHDRAWN

Point-of-Purchase Design

Harvey Offenhartz

 Reinhold Book Corporation

New York   Amsterdam   London

This book is dedicated to

Hal Just

whose friendship and tutelage inspired my career

and to my good friend

Al Mohr

© 1968, Reinhold Book Corporation
All rights reserved
Printed in the United States of America
Library of Congress Catalog Card Number 68-16028

Designed by Myron Hall III
Printed by Halliday Lithograph Corporation
Bound by Publishers Book Bindery
Published by Reinhold Book Corporation
430 Park Avenue, New York, N.Y. 10022

Q 657.15
Of 2p

PREFACE

I have never read a book that has not had one thought or one illustration of some value to me. The journey for knowledge and inspiration is endless. I have discovered some books when I least expected to, and they are constant companions in the search for creation.

So it might be with my book. It has been conceived as a guide and companion for those who seek information about point-of-purchase design. Perhaps with information may come stimulation and inspiration. If so, my objectives will have been well served.

Who then is my reader? Hopefully, all who are involved in the exciting field of point-of-purchase. There is information to be gleaned for salesmen and buyers, advertising, marketing, and sales promotion personnel—all whose very success depends upon successful solutions at the point of purchase.

I have assumed a specific audience and written with it in mind. It consists of the professional designers who have command of the tools of their trade but who, in the course of their careers, have not been involved with point-of-purchase. They are my special audience, for they are needed and welcome at the point of sale.

Throughout the book it will be seen that successful point-of-purchase design requires knowledge that in itself is far afield from design knowledge. It is this information I try to impart; it is this, coupled with the reader's own resources, that will spark effective point-of-purchase design solutions.

I hope the book will open the door to greater understanding of the point-of-purchase medium. Much of what I have to say is fundamental; the rest must come with experience and the solving of practical problems. It is at that point in the designer's experience that I hope my book will be useful as a working companion.

Acknowledgments

There are many people who have helped me in the course of this book. Some are unknown to me except through our correspondence. All have taken the time to help me. Their cooperation and enthusiastic support of my effort have been one of the pleasures of this undertaking. My sincere thanks to the following:

DAN AVERS, D. Avers Advertising
LENNY BARBIERO, Zarember Photography
K. J. BRENNER, Hankscraft Company, Motor Division
EDNA COFFIN CHOO, Point-of-Purchase Advertising Institute
M. D. CLOUD, Thomas A. Schutz Company, Inc.
JAMES F. CONWAY, Mister Softee, Inc.
ROBERT J. COYLE, Johnson & Johnson
EDWARD C. DARDEN JR., Aluminum Company of America
JERRY DARVIN, Jerry Darvin Photography
JEROME DAVIS, Artistic Latex Form Co.
WILLIAM A. DOWSE, Eastern Airlines Incorporated
DONALD A. ELMSLIE, Eastman Kodak Company
ROBERT P. ENGEL, Trans-World Display Corp.
WILLIAM FIELD, Polaroid Corporation
HAROLD FREEMAN, Helena Rubinstein, Inc.
PAUL R. FRITSCH, The Goodyear Tire & Rubber Company
SHIGEO FUKUDA, Shigeo Fukuda, Design
GEORG R. GAERTNER, Georg Gaertner Werbung
RICHARD G. GALEF, The Ravenware Company, Inc.
DAVID GALVER, Spot Magazine, Schwartz Publications, Inc.
JOHN W. GARABRANT, Pepsi-Cola Company
WILLIAM GERSCH, Tel-A-Sign, Inc.
HAROLD B. GOLDRING, Thomson-Leeds, Inc.
MORTON GOLDSHOLL, Goldsholl Associates
G. R. GORRIE, Gorrie Advertising Limited
BERNARD L. GOTTLIEB, Mattel, Inc. Toymakers
BILL GRAHAM, Fillmore Auditorium
R. M. GRAY, Humble Oil & Refining Company
G. WILLIAM GREER, F. Eugene Smith Associates
NORMAN M. HAY, Canadian Corporation for the 1967 World Exhibition
ALLAN HEWITT, Dorothy Gray-Tussy Ltd.
RICHARD M. HIDDING, The Coca-Cola Company
C. JEANNE HOFELICH, Lieberman Associates, Inc.
FRED HOWARD, Howard Displays

KEN ISAACS, Matrix Research Project, Groveland, Illinois
ROBERT M. JONES, RCA Victor Record Division
CARL KAIZAWA, Neographic Art Svs., Tokyo
SAM KAMIN, Neon Products Incorporated
ALEXANDER KAUFMAN, Displaycraft
WILBUR G. KURTZ, The Coca-Cola Company
HARRY LAPOW, Dorothy Gray-Tussy Ltd.
ELLIOTT R. LOEW, P.O.P. Displays, Inc.
FRANCIS X. MAGUIRE, Discover America, Inc.
TOM MALONE, Unimark International
JOHN F. MANFREDI, General Foods Corporation
E. G. MARSHALL, Abbey Goodman Display Ltd., London
DOROTHY A. MAY, Point of Purchase Advertising Institute
DOUGLAS T. McCLURE, Ford Motor Company
THOMAS E. McGANN, Graphic Promotions, Inc.
G. B. McMAUGH, Armour Abrasives Company
ARTHUR MESSINGER, General Foods Corp.
ALFRED V. MOHR, Design 375
CARL ROSEN, Studio Group Inc.
THOMAS J. ROSS, American Airlines
R. R. RORKE, Rohm & Haas Company
WALTER RICHER, Louis Nadelson, Inc.
GEORGE SAPERSTEIN, Visual Graphics Corporation
ROBERT M. SCHAEFFER, National Paper Box Manufacturers Assoc. Inc.
RICHARD R. SCHNETZER, The F & M Schaefer Brewing Co.
BEN J. SEGER, Majestic Creations
RONALD H. TAUB, Creative Displays
ETHEL TAUB, Creative Displays
GEORGE TSCHERNY, Tscherny Design
H. MAC GREGOR TUTTLE, Folding Paper Box Association of America
STAN WALKER, Famous Schools
ANN WALSH, Helena Rubinstein, Inc.
JAMES W.. WALSH JR., Merrill Lynch, Pierce, Fenner & Smith, Inc.
D. H. WATT, The Goodyear Tire & Rubber Company
J. H. WINKLMANN, Westinghouse Appliance Sales & Service Co.
ROBERT G. WOODHEAD, Edinger-Wyckoff Inc.
SAM ZAREMBER, Zarember Photography
ROBERT F. ZOKAS, Ford Motor Company

In addition, I would like to thank Myron Hall III, Carol Isenberg, Jean Koefoed, and Nancy C. Newman of the Reinhold Book Corporation for their cooperation and assistance, and, finally, my family, Carolyn, James, and Lynn.

CONTENTS

INTRODUCTION

The point-of-purchase medium is the vast advertising field most directly related to sales and the consumer. Point-of-purchase materials are those created specifically to engage the consumer at the point of sale. It is in the retail store, away from the mass media, that the consumer and advertiser confront each other—the advertiser with product, the consumer with money (or credit card), the results immediately discernible. The success, indeed, of a point-of-purchase design is measured in dollars generated. The very commercial business of selling—selling with design—is what this book is about.

I need not state that good design is a vital selling tool. Too many sales charts have long proved this; modern management has accepted, if not conceded, it. It is therefore my intention to survey and study the many aspects of the point-of-purchase medium and to discuss these in terms of design.

The first section is a visual survey of point-of-purchase expressions open to the designer, from cut-case display to total selling environment. This will provide the language and techniques of point-of-purchase. The second section discusses design as applied to display and its related graphic problems. It is hoped that the two sections will play back upon each other, giving an understanding of total visual merchandising.

1
HISTORY OF
POINT-OF-PURCHASE

Point-of-purchase advertising is an ancient form of communication. The antecedents of modern point-of-purchase are found in Europe. There is a direct link to our sign industry in the very early tradesmen's signs, which have been traced back to the early Roman Empire. Various signs are mentioned in Roman writings, and actual remnants have been excavated in the ruins of Herculaneum and Pompeii.

It is not until the Middle Ages that more information about these signs becomes available. With the growth of trade and the resulting increase in the number of shops, the need for individual identification developed. With a highly illiterate society, obvious symbols had to be used. Most often these were actual models of products, such as plows, keys, gloves, and kettles. Generally the signs were made of wood or metal. In the case of signboards that illustrated the subject, artists were employed to paint the sign. Smiths embellished the supporting arms of brackets with intricate scrollwork and motifs, unwittingly forming the first collaboration between artist and craftsman and thereby, perhaps, the first point-of-purchase workshop.

As trade grew more competitive, signs grew larger and more elaborate. During the sixteenth and seventeenth centuries in England, they reached gigantic proportions. Some unfortunately fell on passers-by, resulting, in 1762, in a statute requiring signs to be taken down and permanently affixed on storefronts. A commission was established to implement this ruling, which must be the historical precedent and justification for current government regulation of advertising.

With the general acceptance and use of building and street numbers, the need for this kind of sign and signboard declined. The most famous ones still with us today are the barber pole, the pawnshop's three golden balls, and the less-used pestle and mortar. To some degree, these European symbols were carried to the United States, where the most unusual point-of-sale symbol created was the cigar-store Indian. Tobacco was the gift of the American Indian, and he was the most logical symbol, whereas in England, the popular tobacconist's symbol was the Highlander. The period from 1840 to 1880 was the high point in the manufacturing and display of wooden Indians.

The famous cigar-store Indian was hand-carved, usually from white pine, at the rate of one foot a day. It took another day for each foot of painting to be completed. Therefore, delivery of a six-foot Indian usually took twelve days (depending on the supplier). The more competently rendered Indians were probably done by craftsmen who had been carvers of ship's figures. The typical figure was dressed in tanned buckskin, knee-length shirt, belt, leggings, and moccasins. He usually wore a feathered headdress and a kilt of tobacco leaves or feathers, and held in one hand a package of cigars. The carver took many liberties with the details, embellishing for his own pleasure. Thus a romanticized but unknown tribesman was created, who to the present day intrigues many a collector.

With the introduction of Turkish tobacco, a Turk in flowing robes and a turban became another tobacconist's symbol. The last symbol during the waning years of shop figures was a gentleman rendered in the fashion of the day. He wore a checkered jacket, grey slacks, and a bowler hat, and his manner and expression suggested those of a "gentleman." He was displayed prominently in front of fine haberdasheries.

Within the store itself, the merchant created his own signs and sales aids. These were generally hand-lettered signs placed over the particular merchandise, or a blackboard on which he listed daily specials. It is interesting that in the United States in the early days, about 1800, most sales in the general store were made by bartering. Customers exchanged produce for clothing and other needs. The merchandise was not arranged with any deliberate planning. Since few people in the farm areas were literate, the only form of advertisement in the store consisted of brand names inscribed on the barrels which held the major commodities, i.e. crackers, flour, and tea. Just the

dividing of different kinds of merchandise for display in separate parts of one store was a major innovation.

The very earliest in-store fixtures that were sent in by manufacturers were signs, usually printed on metal, which were mounted on wooden frames. Sometimes a permanent fixture in which to store the merchandise was created. A good example is the Humphrey's Remedy display, in which medicines for almost every known disease (and several not yet discovered) were stored.

It is hard to believe that stores were so primitive less than one hundred years ago, when we are surrounded by the wealth of goods in retail stores today. Glass storefronts were not used extensively until the middle of the nineteenth century. Neon

signs only became available in 1922. Thus, within a period of fifty years, there was progress in the organization of the store, the use of glass fronts, and neon lighting. The progress was slow and hesitant. For example, window display signs did not come into their own until before World War I. Prior to this, merchants were content to place as much merchandise in their store windows as could fit, ignoring the bulky, cluttered effect. Their attempts to advertise merchandise and attract customers had the overstuffed look of present-day pawnshops.

The history of point-of-purchase display is very directly related to that of retailing. As retailing has become more sophisticated in its merchandising techniques and requirements, so have point-of-purchase selling aids.

The Turk in flowing robes is another tobacconist's symbol. On the pedestal is additional signage for Navy Smoking and Chewing Tobacco, Cremo Cigars, and Old Virginia Cheroots. The Stationery, Toy and Candy store window boasts many signs, including ones for Esterbrook Pens and Carter's Inks. The Esterbrook symbol (in the entrance) is in the shape of a pen nib. A permanent sign for Copenhagen Snuff and signs for other tobaccos are placed wherever space is available. Judging from the metal toys in the window, this photograph dates from 1905-1910.

A cigar-store Indian, about 1895. Typically, the brave has his hand to his forehead. Note the outdoor display case, holding greeting cards and toys; such cases were often found in front of retail stores.

This stationery store was photographed in 1896 or 1897. Among the many signs is one for the sale of the Edison Mimeograph, which makes 3000 copies. Note the sign for a First Class Regular 7 Course Dinner of Farinaceous Food for 25¢. The object on the steps appears to be a replica ink bottle display. Stock certificates are for sale; one hesitates to think of the appreciation of an 1897 investment.

A Coca-Cola illustration captures the look of the ideal drug-store fountain about 1903. The illustration was used on a counter card placed behind the fountain.

The interior of an A & P store about 1890 shows that the merchandise is neatly organized and displayed for easy identification — an innovation in its time.

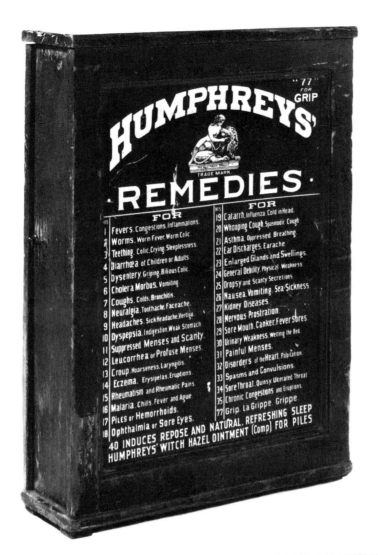

The Humphrey's Remedies display might have F.D.A. trouble today, but it is a classic storage cabinet of its time.

There is, as we are discovering, a charm to old signs and displays. Many can still be found by those with time, energy, and inclination. Below are but a few of the pieces collected by Mr. William Hayett of Hayett Displays.

A Coca-Cola syrup dispenser and the famous original Coca-Cola Tiffany lamp.

The Coca-Cola calendars are a study in feminine idolatry. The 1901 calendar is typographically unusual: it is an exceptionally advanced piece for its time.

A very early sampling ticket, or free coupon give-away, for one glass of Coca-Cola.

This die-cut window display, produced around 1907, is an early example of a window display supplied by the advertiser to the retail store. Note that the Coca-Cola inscribed glasses are already in use.

At the turn of the century, amid the clutter of worded signage, Goodyear distributed a simple tacker sign to its dealers. It simply stated, ''Agent, Goodyear Rubber Tires, Akron, Ohio.'' It was distributed to blacksmiths who were exclusively franchised to install Goodyear tires on carriage wheels. The winged foot appeared on the sign, and has been a symbol of Goodyear since the company's founding.

The motorized vehicle and the horse-drawn wagon shown date from approximately 1910. It is of interest to note that both products are still vigorously advertised in the point-of-purchase medium.

The package has long been its own message. Often a container from which portions of the product were sold, it carried its own sales story. Large display type was its greatest asset, since the company name was the recognizable identification for a literate populace, but a distinctive shape was another advantage. Towles Log Cabin Syrup, introduced in 1887, is such an example. The other packages are typical containers of the time.

The Elgin Motor Company sign is the ultimate expression in signage of its era. Besides its inherent value, it is a fantastic prototype of contemporary Pop art. We have begun today to collect artifacts of the American past, many of which are products of the point-of-purchase medium. This phenomenon is amusing to those of us who are producers of contemporary point-of-purchase materials. Perhaps you should keep something of what you do today, for it may well be a collector's item tomorrow.

It is clear from the brief survey of old point-of-purchase material that the roots of this medium are an integral part of our economic history. Signs and like material were the natural medium of advertising until the advent of the mass media of print and television, which today receive the bulk of advertising dollars and consideration. But it is still at the point of purchase that the sale is concluded and it is there that the advertiser is most vulnerable. It is there that we are called upon to influence the buying decision with all the means at our disposal. These means are the subject of this book.

2
POINT-OF-PURCHASE EXPRESSIONS

DISPLAY MERCHANDISERS

Point-of-purchase is an advertising method in itself. It has its own means of expression, its own restrictions, and an unlimited potential for growth and expression. It serves many functions. It states the brand or company name, reminding the consumer of the product or company. It can tie in visually with national advertising, thereby reinforcing the advertiser's message right in the retail store. Point-of-purchase advertising can attract consumer attention by means of its own graphics or physical presence, thereby stimulating the buying impulse. Finally, it can act as a source of information and education.

Point-of-purchase merchandisers display products at the retail outlet. Their importance has increased with the growth of retailing and the needs of mass marketing. The expansion of self-service stores, and the resulting change in consumer buying habits, have contributed to the development of point-of-purchase materials. More often than not, unplanned buying decisions are made in the store, and the effective display of merchandise is the deciding factor in the consumer's choice.

The structures in which advertising messages are presented, often referred to as displays, are the vehicles out of which the merchandise is presented and sold. They take many forms, from a simple cut-case corrugated display to an elaborate plastic unit. Each form is a result of the marketing function of the display.

The following pages present these displays and the reasons for their use as marketing tools. The means of expression change with industry and retail use; the shapes and forms change as new materials and techniques are developed. But the fundamental purpose of point-of-purchase advertising remains constant: to communicate a message and thereby stimulate sales.

Promotional Displays

In the broad sense, all displays are "promotional." But this word is specifically used to indicate a display which is designed for use only for the duration of a particular sales campaign, in contrast to units which are designed for use for an indefinite period of time.

Generally speaking, promotional pieces have a short life expectancy (several weeks), and therefore the materials used are usually corrugated board, paperboard, or inexpensive plastics. The promotional budget and the number of units to be manufactured determine the choice of material. The higher the dollar value of the merchandise in the display, the greater the amount of money that can be budgeted for the display. Again, more displays can be manufactured for the dollar when there are 30,000 units being made than when there are 5,000 units. Once the requirements of budget have been met, the form and graphics of the promotion can be determined.

There are literally thousands of promotions created annually. In addition to stable items, new products are continually being introduced or old products repackaged, and all are competing for shelf and display space. There are special wholesale incentives as well as consumer incentives which motivate acceptance of the promotion. Marketing objectives and problems are indeed the concern of the designer if he is to create displays that have selling value. Selling value includes more than showing merchandise in a decorated display.

The simplest kind of promotional displays are those that organize merchandise that is without its own structure. Many fast-selling products are sold directly from their shipping cases. These are called "cut-case" displays, because the dealer cuts along the dotted line to remove the top part of the carton and expose the merchandise. He then simply stacks the cartons, thus getting the merchandise off the shelves and onto a favorable spot on the selling floor. Riser cards with appropriate sales messages are usually included; these add a decorative touch to the cartons, thereby creating the effects of a display.

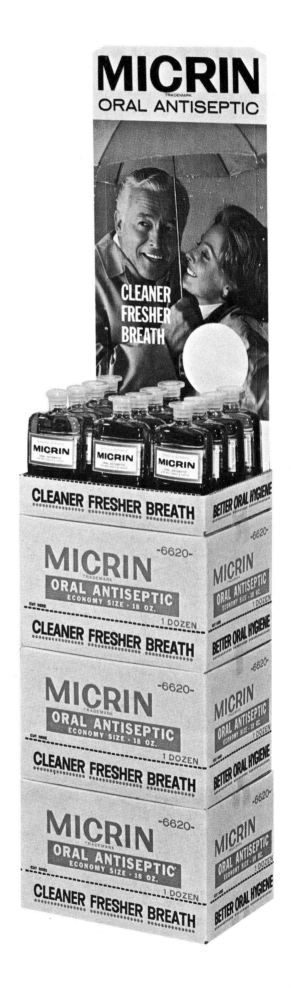

The White Satin Gin graphics are immediately identifiable. Strong typography and symbols and bold color project the message clearly. Note the continuity of the graphics on a corrugated bin with pole topper and on a counter display. The counter unit is in the original shipping case, cut along perforations to reveal the contents. The riser card is inserted to complete the display. The visual strength of the riser card more than offsets the possible scruffiness of the case (due to shipping), and is an inexpensive way to solve a display problem. This unit could also sit on top of several unopened cases and would thus become a floor stand.

An example of such a floor stand is the Micrin unit of Johnson and Johnson.

The "dump bin" is a bin-shaped holder, designed to stand on the floor, which contains merchandise in random order. It is so called because the merchandise can be "dumped" in from the shipping case, thereby saving the time necessary to stack it neatly. Equally important, the random display of the product encourages a "help-yourself" attitude on the part of the consumer.

The Brands display is an actual wire duplicate of the shape of the product. This seemingly simple unit holds a minimum of 450 jars of the product and serves its function well in supermarkets in Great Britain. The techniques of point-of-sale are international when properly applied.

The Quaker Oats display dramatizes the carton and uses its super size as storage for the product. The carton, a memorable one in households, is utilized as an effective self-identifier.

The Jell-O Parfait mix is enticingly presented on the pole topper, but the construction of the dump bin is of particular interest to us. It has been constructed in the shape of a parfait — no small accomplishment with corrugated board.

A "pole display" is a display mounted to a footed pole. It is designed to carry the advertising message and to be used with a large amount of merchandise. The sign carrying the message is called the pole topper. Pole toppers are often three-dimensional and are elaborate both graphically and in their construction.

The great advantage of the pole display is that it can be used with large quantities of merchandise, thereby calling attention to the product and creating a unified display. The merchandise is either stacked or stands in its own shipping case, which is cut open to reveal its contents. As consumers we are most familiar with the pole display because of its wide use in supermarkets.

The Burry pole toppers are representative of supermarket graphics. They are light in approach, colorful, and decorative. They use stylized illustrations appealing to adults as well as to children. The stagecoach unit is somewhat elaborate to set up and was designed for installation by the advertiser's salesman.

Not unlike the Burry graphics is the Dixie Picnic Pick Ups topper. Because it features a variety of picnic and barbecue items, the supermarket manager has a display around which he can show not only Dixie cups and plates but also food, soft drinks, and relishes. Thus, the display helps him to move many items and increases its selling value to him.

The Sylvania pole topper offers the consumer a "send-away" premium of Betty Crocker Cookbooks, an additional incentive for the consumer to purchase Sylvania light bulbs.

Utica Club's mug is an inflated vinyl replica of the mug used in the company's national advertising. The Santa hat is a continuation at the point of sale of the playful approach taken by the advertiser.

The Schaefer lighthouse is battery-operated, with the light going on and off. Its theme is to encourage the sale of two six-packs rather than the one six-pack that the customer might normally buy. During the Christmas season, Schaefer uses a holiday gift pack. Note the use of corrugated feet rather than wire at the base of the pole. Both pole toppers carry the same message, one at a lesser cost.

Motion is often used with pole toppers, providing them with more interest and action. The Hamms Beer units are battery-operated moving displays. The bear and small animals are vacuum-formed in plastic.

The mobile has become a form of our times. The concept of the mobile has been applied commercially in manifold ways. In the supermarket, the mobile is an ideal identifier that can be used with or without products. Suspended from the ceiling, it does not compete for precious floor space. A mobile, such as this Tang spaceship, functions similarly to a pole topper.

It is not only in supermarkets that the use of the mobile is valuable. The Romika mobile is part of promotional material prepared in Germany for shoe stores there. The Venetian theme promotes the use of leisure shoes during travel.

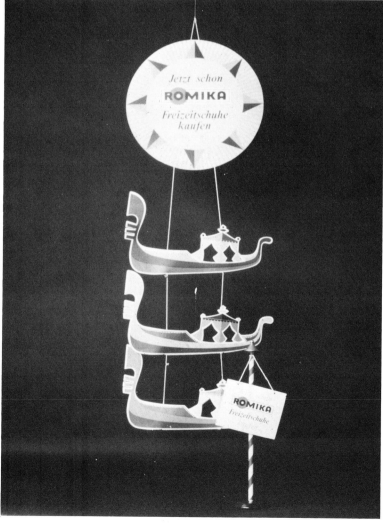

Some merchandise comes in its own promotional floor stand, and the dealer has only to set it up. These floor stands are another simple way for the manufacturer to get his merchandise onto the selling floor.

The Leilani Hawaiian Rum unit is an excellent example of a package label, itself an exciting visual, making a striking display. The photography immediately suggests the essence of Hawaii; the display all but puts a lei around your neck.

This Kent unit evokes the nostalgic feeling of Christmas. The carriage is cut diagonally to reveal more of the carton when the display is fully loaded. Because it was anticipated that the unit would have to hold competitive brands of cigarettes or not be used at all, Kent used a general message reader and omitted brand identification.

31

One of the ways to ensure getting floor space for your product is to send the merchandise to the dealer with some kind of special promotional offer to the consumer or a special incentive to the dealer.

The Whip 'n Chill display has a free recipe book offer, with a sample of the book attached to the display for study and an offer pad with the instructions on how to obtain the recipe book. This type of merchandiser is referred to as a "send-away premium." The Johnson and Johnson display offers a similar incentive.

The "Jell-O Treasure Hunt" is another example of a send-away premium. In this instance, the consumer receives up to $1.00 for returning a quantity of Jell-O Gelatin cartons. While the rules and games vary, merchandisers of this kind are additional incentives for stores to use displays, and they stimulate sales. These promotions are usually backed by print and television advertising, but can only be consummated at the point of sale. The plastic boat that holds the merchandise is in itself an inexpensive stock item that ties in perfectly with the promotion.

The Jell-O Jackpot display is unmistakable in its meaning. The consumer matches a coupon found in her home-delivered magazine with the display, to determine if she is a winner. The coupon itself is redeemable with the purchase of Jell-O. The contest originates in the home and motivates the consumer to look for the display in her food store; the fostering of traffic in the store and the additional sale of the product add to the store's acceptance of this promotion.

This Jell-O display holds a mold that is given free with each purchase. This kind of promotion, known as a "near-pack incentive," aids in stimulating sales.

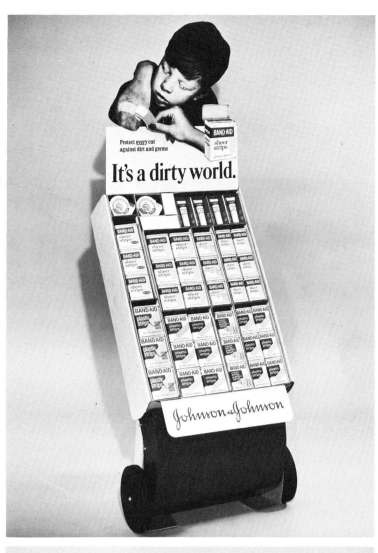

Among the many ways to help sell a promotion to the store is the "dealer incentive," or "dealer loader." The display is designed around some useful take-home unit for the dealer, such as a table, cart, or grill.

Three Johnson and Johnson promotions effectively employ dealer incentives — a patio cart, canvas chair, and lawn seed sprinkler — in their design. The graphics of the decorative illustration as well as the photography are particularly effective in conveying their message.

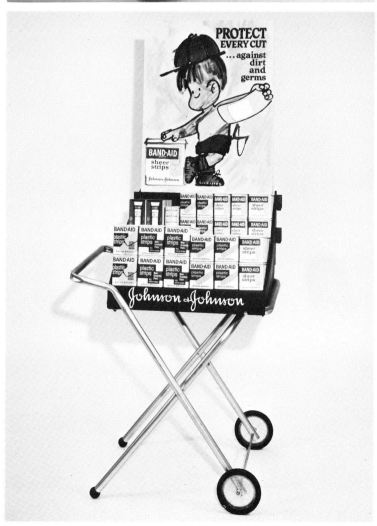

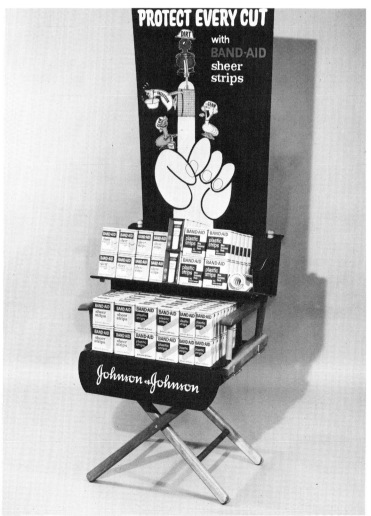

The consumer's use of fruit with Dream Whip is the basis for this promotion. The Dream Whip wire unit was designed to sit high above the boxes of strawberries, in the fruit department of the store. Its display at this point makes it a strong impulse item, with an additional money-back incentive. There is no forgetting the topping when you buy the strawberries. This cooperative promotion between the two companies is an example of a "tie-in" promotion. Often tie-ins feature money-saving combinations, or related items, such as toothbrush and toothpaste or razor and shaving cream. Products may or may not be manufactured by different companies.

Sometimes, to secure a large display area, the advertiser will create a generic display featuring related items, many of which are not his own merchandise. Naturally, those items are non-competitive. The General Foods Holiday Baking Center is an example of such an "altruistic" display.

The Yardley display holds various products, yet achieves an uncluttered look. Since the colors of all the products can be seen, a shade chart is needed only for the lipsticks; it is shown just in front of them. The London Look advertising theme of Yardley is evoked in the display. The base of the unit is vacuum-formed; the rest of the display consists of lithographed sheets mounted to paperboard. This is a highly successful display, which Yardley has duplicated many times in similar forms.

As can be seen from the preceding example, cosmetic displays do everything but gift wrap the purchase. In the drugstore the consumer often selects her products unaided by a cosmetician or clerk. The display must tell her and show her what she needs to know. And it must do this amid similar displays offering similar merchandise. Therefore, in cosmetics in particular, you find promotions identical in theme and appearance to national advertising campaigns. The objective is to show the consumer at the point of sale the same message she saw in *Vogue* or *Harpers Bazaar*.

If the point of purchase is a drugstore rather than a supermarket, there is little floor space. Therefore the manufacturer sends in structures to hold his merchandise on counters. Again, their function is to get the merchandise off the shelves and in a place easily accessible to the consumer.

Delightful, whimsical Tussy displays encourage the sale of the equally whimsical packaging. These stocking fillers for Christmas are displayed during the busy holiday season when drugstores abound with displays and gift items. Their restraint and charm are a welcome sight at any time of the year.

A similar approach was created at Helena Rubinstein for an equally playful stocking stuffer.

BE AN ANGEL... GIVE HER HELENA RUBINSTEIN'S **HEAVEN SENT** PERFUME SPRAY 225 SPRAYS $2²⁵

Excitement begins with *Midnight* cream perfume $1.50

Midnight an enchanting, bewitching fragrance

Midnight purse perfume $2.00

Permanent Displays

Often an advertiser will provide a permanent selling structure to the dealer. Permanent units serve essentially the same functions as their promotional counterparts, but they are meant to last for a much longer time, and therefore more money can be spent in their creation. They are designed to ensure a permanent space in the store for the advertiser's product on the shelf, counter, or floor. While many permanent units carry promotional items, most can be used beyond the extent of the promotion. Because they are durable, they can be restocked with merchandise. Thus, the object of the permanent merchandiser is to ensure the favorable display of the product for an indefinite period of time.

Permanent units range from something as simple as a wire rack to actual structures in the store.

Three devices for organizing merchandise on a shelf are "spring loaders," "shelf extenders," and "shelf dividers." These are good ways of ensuring proper display of small products on crowded shelves.

Johnson and Johnson Baby Soap is displayed in a two-level spring loader. A heavy spring pushes the merchandise forward as it is removed, ensuring the constant display of the product at the front of the shelf.

The shelf extender, usually a small tray, is fastened or clamped to a shelf and projects from it, thus increasing the space available. The Crew display is such an example.

The Florient shelf divider arranges the product into neat rows, allowing a row for each type of mist. This vacuum-formed plastic divider is an inexpensive and efficient way of presenting similarly packaged merchandise that varies by content; women's hair-coloring products are often organized in this manner.

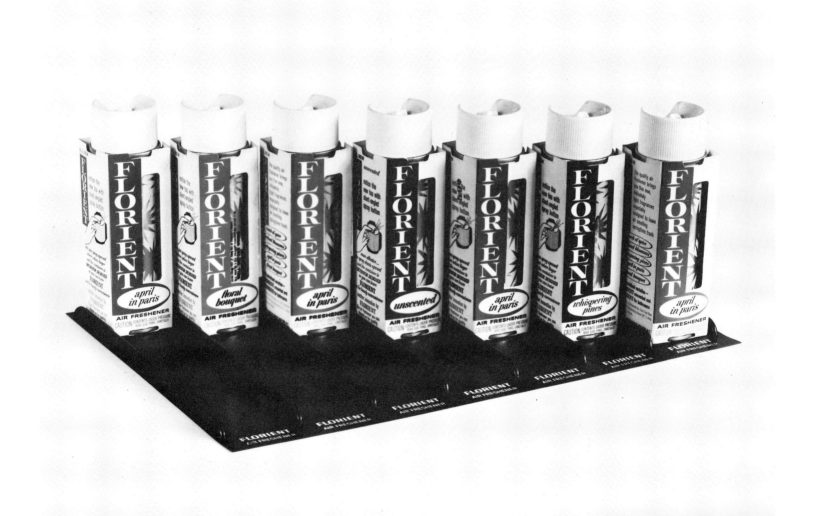

Permanent display racks are often supplied to the store to aid in the display of merchandise, particularly when it is difficult to show. Some are designed to organize material on a shelf. For example, the Good Season's Salad Dressing mix is a wire display, with dividers between the packages, organizing the products for easy identification.

The Tuffy wire rack is a miniature dump bin for use on supermarket shelves and effectively displays a difficult-to-store product.

The Clairol Hair Care Center display is a sturdy wire rack that aids the dealer to display hair-coloring and hair care products in one unit, thereby encouraging sales of related items. The chart at the bottom is a hair-color chart. While this is a counter unit, larger display fixtures have been provided to stores for the purpose of displaying Clairol hair products.

The counter is an ideal selling space, and permanent counter units are the advertiser's means of utilizing this space.

The Scripto palette display is vacuum-formed and conveniently holds 144 pens in a minimum amount of space. A pad is provided to test the writing of the pen. The pens are shown in their original shipping containers; the dealer can easily replace each carton as it is sold, thereby restocking the display effortlessly.

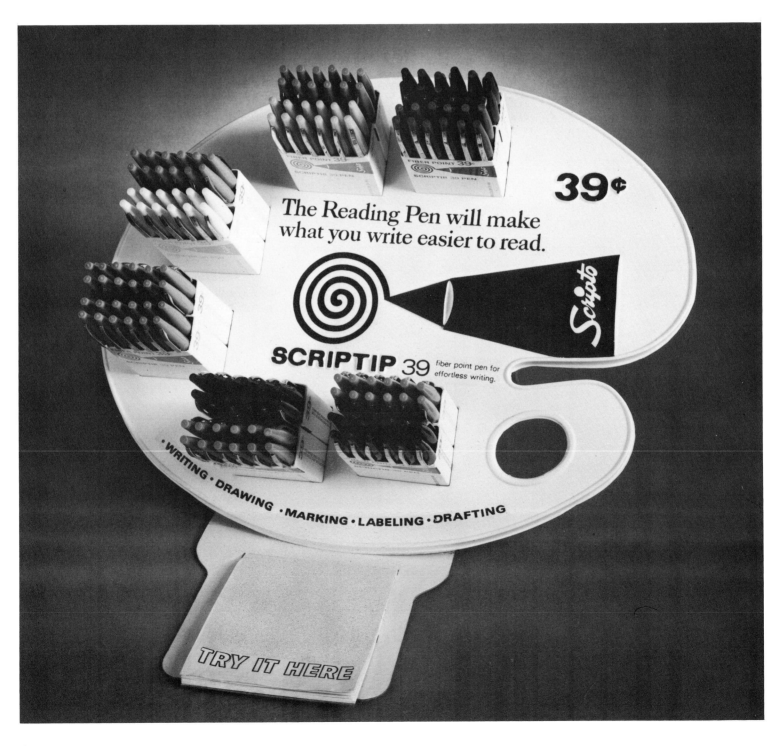

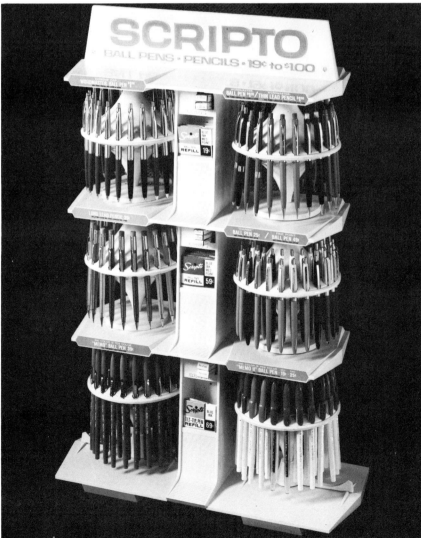

The other two displays are injection-molded for greater durability and permanence. The holders revolve, exposing all pens and pencils to the consumer, for easy access and choice. The larger unit stores pen refills and leads, making a complete Scripto center in a very small area.

The palette display would be classified as a semipermanent display. Because of its structure, this display's life expectancy might be the sell-out of the gross of pens. The injection-molded displays are permanent units. They are designed for use over a longer period of time than a promotional piece, hopefully defined as one year. The structure and value of the display to the dealer determines the true permanence of any display. Obviously, the most elaborate display will not last a month if it serves no function. By the same token, units defined as semipermanent have lingered long after the advertiser's expectation, because they moved merchandise. Salability is the criterion, not the cost of the unit.

The introduction of the new Lightworks line of cosmetics geared to the youth market required a unique package and display. The black and white package is smart and contemporary, and the display projects the line without imposing upon it. The background is stainless steel, reflecting light and the packages.

This display was designed for many months of use. The blank holes in the bottom tray allow for the possibility of additional lipstick shades being introduced. Since this was a new line, actual products, out of their cartons, were mounted in place on the display. In addition, lipsticks were provided in the base for the consumer to test colors before buying, and color-shade charts were mounted on each shelf.

The riser card gives a three-dimensional illusion; it was the first use of this technique in the cosmetic industry. This was achieved by photographing the products with a special 3D camera. The resulting ektachrome art was lithographed, and a lenticular lens was laminated to the printed sheet. The lenticular lens creates the three-dimensional quality. The riser was then permanently attached to the display.

Three-dimensional printing is making gigantic strides at this date and will soon be economical enough to be commonplace in displays. The object will be to use it creatively and not as a gimmick or device.

Blister-pack cards are usually displayed by hanging on a wire from pegboard displays. To show a blister pack in a counter display requires a unique solution. This slotted unit of injection-molded plastic solves the problem creatively for Cutex. While it may seem a simple solution, any designer who has worked with a dozen bulky blister-pack cards will appreciate the result.

The Turquoise wire display with clear, injection-molded bins can accommodate various quantities of pencils in many arrangements. It is easily serviced by the dealer and is equally accessible to the consumer.

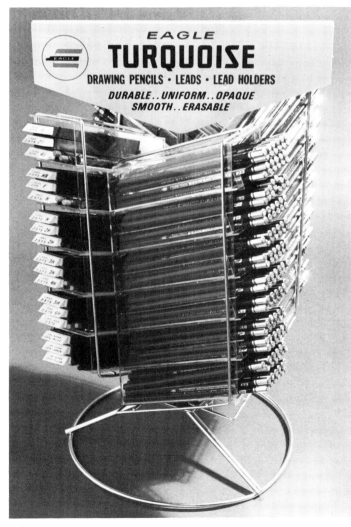

Kodak's "Stand . . . and Expand" film dispenser is an extremely versatile modular unit. The individual units interlock by means of channels on each side of the dispensers, so that any number of units can be used in a group. Plastic dividers fit into grooves inside each dispenser, varying to accommodate different sizes of film cartons. The basic unit is injection-molded, and has a clear plastic sheet that covers the entire front, except for the bottom space from which the film is removed. This is a good example of a "gravity-feed" unit. The unit can be used standing or hanging on a wall.

Space in travel agencies has become increasingly difficult to obtain, and airlines face marketing problems similar to those of consumer-goods' manufacturers in bringing their message to the attention of the consumer. The El Al shopping guide, a wood and pressed-paperboard display, holds travel folders. Moreover, its dial can be turned to reveal a list of commodities for which each city is known, thereby engaging the interest of the would-be traveller.

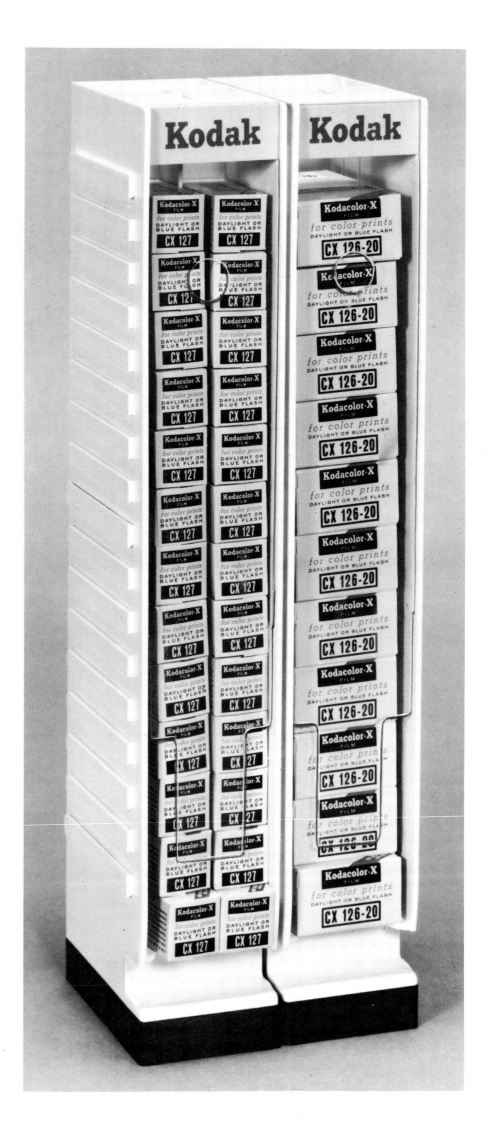

A permanent cosmetic display functions as a reference on counters of the advertiser's lipstick or make-up line. In addition to displaying the product, it has color charts showing the range of colors in the line. The back of the display stores merchandise for the dealer. The elaborateness of the displays attests to the importance attributed to them by the advertiser.

The Clairol unit is an attractive one. Seemingly constructed of ash wood, it is actually injection-molded plastic, technically an achievement of high merit. The unit gives the feeling of being "at home" on a woman's dressing table, and the effect in a drugstore is quite personal to the purchaser.

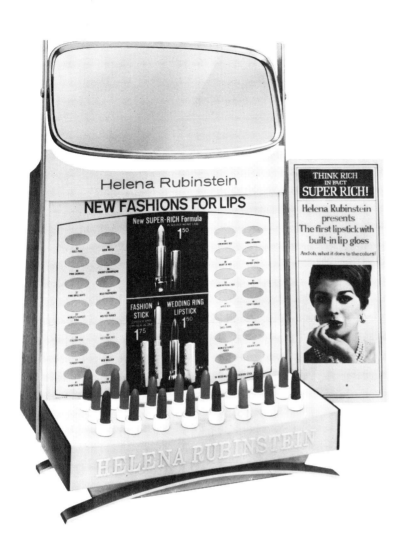

The Helena Rubinstein unit offers both a tester and shade chart, and has the added attraction of a movable mirror. The mirror is a stopper, since it can be seen at eye level when the display is on the counter. The woman can remove the lipstick and test it on her hand. This gives her the opportunity to see the lipstick shade against her own skin tone, as well as to feel the texture of the product. The unit is constructed of simulated walnut and has brass-plated sides, legs, and mirror. The tester unit is injection-molded plastic and is detachable for use away from the display, if necessary. The tester part could thus be used in department stores that would not accommodate the larger unit.

The Revlon Nail Polish display functions in much the same manner as the other units, except that it is also a merchandiser. It functions as a permanent merchandiser and may well be the forerunner of similar merchandisers, which will do away with units that are only showcases. What may seem a contradiction is really an example of the constant change that takes place on the initiative of the advertiser or the display producer. There is every opportunity for the designer to innovate, both in display design and merchandising technique.

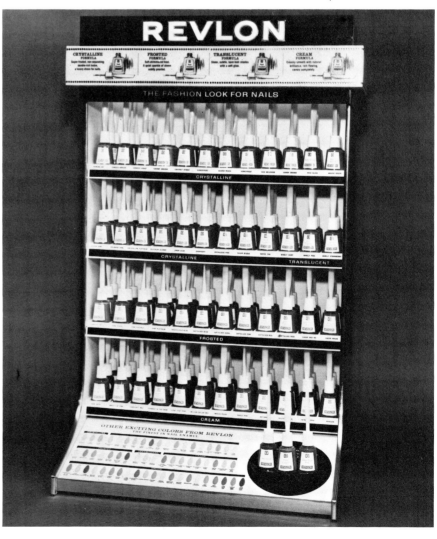

The three-bottle wire unit was used to feature three new Calvert mixes. The medallion shape of the label is repeated in a colorful riser card.

The display of individual Mattel dolls was solved by the creation of "Show-case" doll stands. The stand can show dolls either standing or sitting. Inter-changeable headers are provided to identify individual dolls. The stands are equally versatile in their use in the store: they can be hung on a wall, stacked on a counter or in a window, or placed on gondola ends. The showcase combined with a canopy makes a complete Mattel center, unmistakable to the consumer seeking the famous "Barbie Doll" and its family.

The Citizen's Watch display was created in Japan for use at trade shows in the western world. A Hokusai print was selected as a symbol of Japan which would be recognizable to Westerners. Bamboo shoots were mounted to a base that held native black sand, completing an effect that is both traditional and contemporary at the same time.

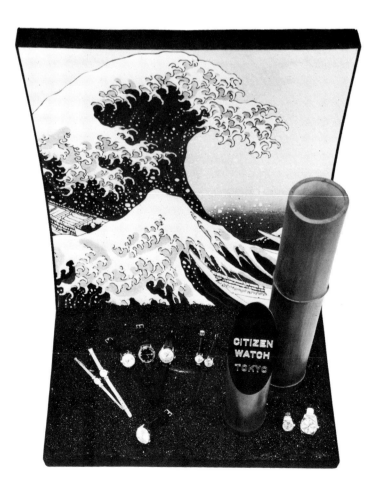

In the hope of maintaining a private selling area in the store, the advertiser provides the dealer with permanent floor structures.

Pepsi-Cola supplied supermarkets with this ten-foot revolving replica of its bottle. It stores cartons and provides for the display of related snack items.

To feature refrigerated products, a display can be designed for use above the freezer unit, near competing products. But with the mobile freezer unit, Palm Ice Cream could be displayed any place in the store, thus being isolated from other brands. The unit carries its own visual, which can be changed with each promotion. While this is a costly display, the tremendous sales increase of Palm products justified the initial investment.

Babes in Toyland stocks various books and games in a clear presentation. The riser sets the tone of the theme without competing with the products themselves. The drum under "Babes in Toyland" is a focal point of the display due to the use of light and motion. Heat waves generated by an electric bulb activate fins (similar to the action of wind on a pin wheel), causing the drum to revolve.

The Foster Grant Suntower display unit makes use of the company's own plastics capability to create a modern look. This display is made of reinforced polystyrene core and a clear crystal polystyrene outer wall. Each model can hold as many as five dozen pairs of sunglasses. The sunglasses seem to float in mid air, though they are actually attached to a clear plastic holder. The construction design features interchangeable modules with headers highlighting the company's current advertising campaign; the headers can be inserted at any level. This smart, flexible floor unit revolves for complete access to its merchandise.

The cone-shaped Calvert display is a modular unit that was adapted from an existing flower planter mold. The holders can be used individually, or collectively, as shown. The vertical shape uses little floor space. The display was designed to be seen from both sides, with a double-mounted riser card. New riser cards are periodically issued for use on the display.

Successful advertising coupled with a successful product does not always mean success at the point of sale, particularly when that could be any environment from a toy store to a hardware store, supermarket, sporting goods store, or discount house. While the consumer may be seeking a specific brand, he may not be able to find it.

Mattel created a display that solved this problem. It developed a Mattel canopy that could be used on a wall, on a post, over a gondola, or as a floor stand. This system is flexible enough in application to fit in any retail environment that sells toys. The canopy is made of a durable metal foil, silk-screened in red and gold. It comes with seven identifiers, each imprinted with the name of a Mattel doll or toy. In addition to supplying the canopy to the stores, Mattel provided the hardware necessary for its use in any manner decided upon by the dealer. The example illustrated shows it as a floor stand.

The Lee's Carpet Clamp Waterfall mobile display is an effective way to show and sell carpet samples in a small area. It provides for instant display and comparison of samples. Each sample can be easily removed for horizontal on-floor demonstration.

The Guilstan Show-Go wall units are made up of individual sections, each with an illuminated header. They can be used as a wall unit, as shown, or individually. The sections allow for the organization of carpets by quality, color, texture, or price, and hold from two to eighty samples. The desk and transparency section is optional.

Notions are hard to store and equally difficult to display. The Riviera unit does both extremely well in a small (thirty-inch-square) floor area. The four individual rotating display sections turn to expose more products. They hold over a thousand carded hair ornaments, with 192 different facings. Velvet-covered display rolls near the top of the unit hold headbands. Note the mirrors mounted on all sides. The base has two drawers for additional storage of inventory.

The Westinghouse display, made of wood, wire, and masonite, was designed to show huge pieces of furniture. The units are individual, but their use together makes a more unusual and effective display.

The General Electric display was developed in Canada for use there. It was designed to be shown on a portable television stand that dealers were also selling. The base, selling card, and moving topper all contributed to a unified display. The circle rotates 180 degrees.

Often material is found at the point of purchase which does not hold merchandise, but which is displayed near it. This material is designed to advertise a product in a special way, or to be an aid to the consumer and/or the dealer. Thus we find these special point-of-purchase materials ranging from something as simple as a counter mat, menu cover, or change holder with the advertiser's name on it to more sophisticated aids such as a light box for viewing color slides. The need for these materials ensures their success.

The Antique Bourbon series of Hall-of-Fame champions is a symbol of the brand. Each season a new athlete is added to the collection. Shown here in molded rubber replicas, these units are about four and a half feet tall and are used in store interiors. The unit shown with the product is a porcelain version and is painted in nine colors; this unit is distributed to taverns and stores.

Heat-sealed vinyl inflatables are currently used as giant replicas of products. Approximately forty inches tall, they accurately duplicate the product in color and form. Easily carried, they inflate simply, like a plastic beach ball. These examples illustrate a Snow Crop Orange Juice can, the famous Coca-Cola bottle, and the J & B Scotch bottle. The J & B inflatable is shown against a real quart bottle. The inflatables are practically weightless, and can be displayed easily on counters, windows, and floors, or suspended from the ceiling.

At this stage in the development of the inflatable it is used most in product replicas. As technological advances are made and the needs of advertisers become more demanding, the inflatable will be used in more complex renditions.

The Helena Rubinstein Eye Make-up tester display was designed for use in department stores. The customer is encouraged to test the product for its color and consistency when applied to her own skin. Units like these are valuable selling aids in stores; the unit and a trained cosmetician can offer considerable aid to the consumer, encouraging multiple sales. The display, lucite with gold hot stamping, is a smart unit compatible with department store fixtures and interiors.

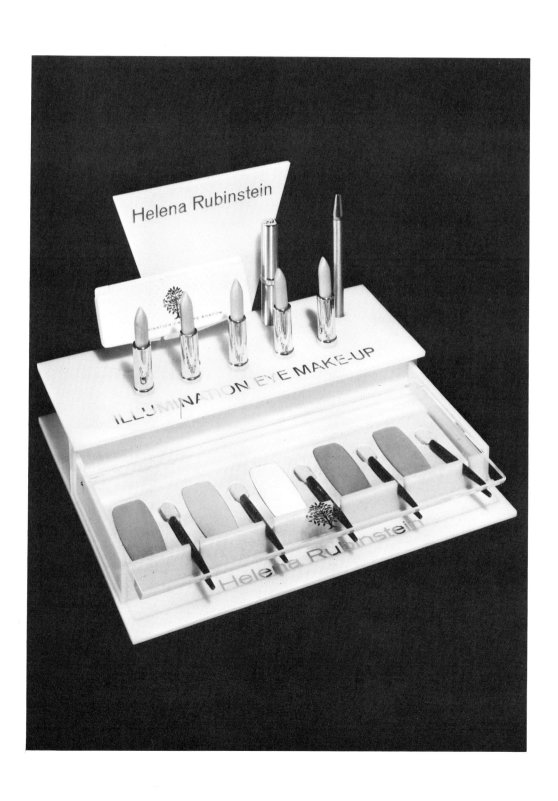

The Kodak unit is an excellent example of the principle of dealer aid as well as consumer aid at the point of purchase. The unit is a wood construction and includes a light box for viewing negatives and transparencies. The information about Kodak color prints provided in the multiringed binder is of immediate value to the consumer in determining his photographic needs. Its value as a workable and useful selling aid cannot be overemphasized.

An equally valuable guide at the point of purchase is the Ford Color and Trim Selection Book. The spiral-bound unit shows actual fabric swatches on one page and specifications on the other. The right side of the book has exterior color samples and outline drawings of each model car on clear acetate. The car selected can then be placed over the flat color to get the effect of the car's appearance. The book is an extremely valuable aid in completing sales.

It is my guess that the reader has utilized one or both of these units at some time as a consumer. Presented in this book, within the framework of our definition of point-of-purchase, they can be seen in a new light.

The principles of the Ford Color and Trim Section Book become an even better selling aid when applied to a permanent display. The Color Center can be used by the customer while browsing in the showroom or by the salesman as a selling tool. Each panel is changeable, thereby adding to the longevity of the unit, and empty space is provided for the storage of booklets and brochures. Note that the application of Ford signage to this display is in keeping with the standards of its sign program discussed on page 119.

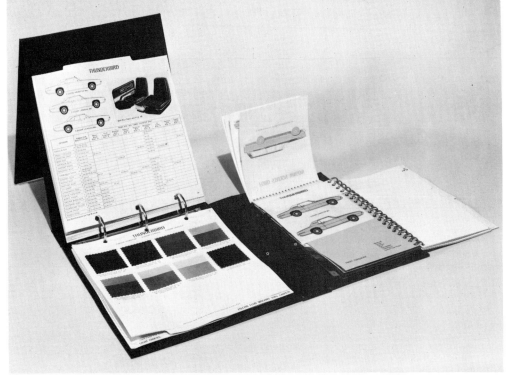

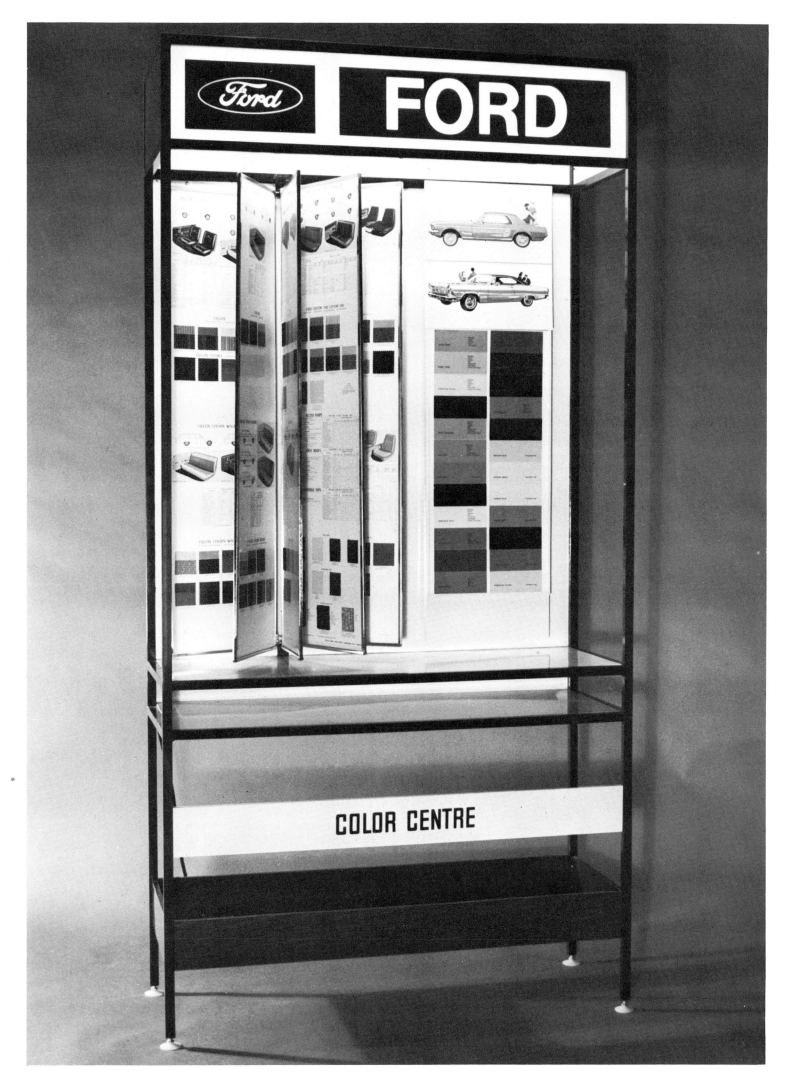

PACKAGES

My discussion of packaging is very specific. I am concerned with examples that fulfill only one function: strong display impact at the point of sale. The graphic problems of these packages are not unlike those of displays and therefore are of concern to us. Thus, although packaging is a specialized field with its own technical problems, it is not a separate design area. Therefore, point-of-purchase involvement may well begin with the package, the graphics of which are the concern of all designers.

A perfect example with which to illustrate the relationship of packaging to point-of-sale is the Polaroid "Swinger" package. The typography and stylized camera illustration are effective in setting the exciting tone of a product planned for the youth market. Three sides of the carton are black and three sides are respectively blue, purple, and green, so that, by mixing or matching colors, an attractive display can be created. This is of particular concern since the camera is sold in many kinds of retail outlets, mostly without Polaroid display units as a background. Thus, the designer solved a marketing problem with graphic excellence.

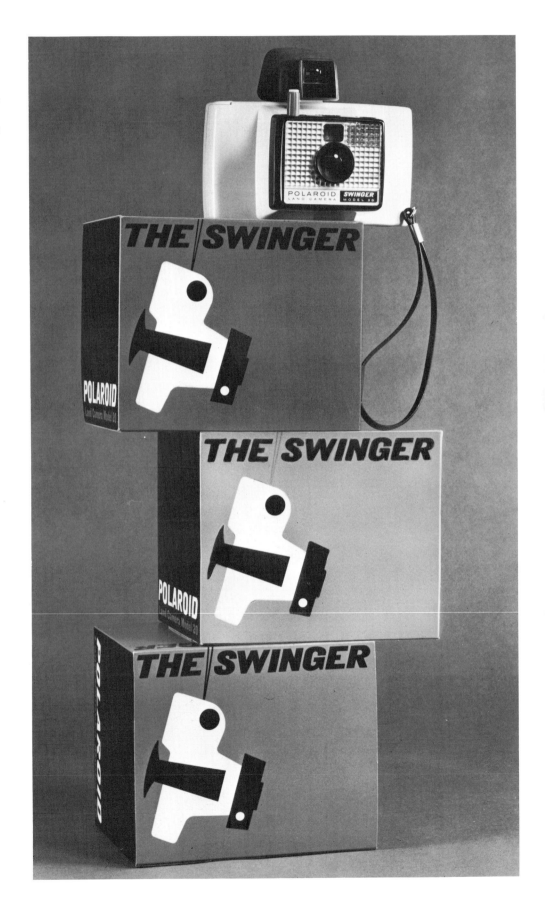

The Old Fitzgerald Venetian decanter was appropriately packaged with a Venetian scene, which was used around the carton. When several cartons were lined up, the entire scene could be re-created. Decorative and unusual, the packages make maximum use of shelf facings.

The Gablinger Beer counter card is an exact duplicate of the Gablinger Beer six-pack; the strong typography and photography worked extraordinarily well in both instances. The message is reinforced many times when the six-packs are stacked, making an exciting package quite different from the graphics of competitive brands.

There is no doubt about the contents of these four cartons. Each in its own way is bold and direct, clearly showing its contents, and creating a strong visual impression on the shelf.

The Clairol packages represent an innovation in marketing hair colorings. Heretofore, the consumer had to refer to a hair-color chart before making her selection, but charts at the point of purchase become dog-eared and tend to disappear. By showing the actual shade on the package, Clairol could sell more directly to the consumer.

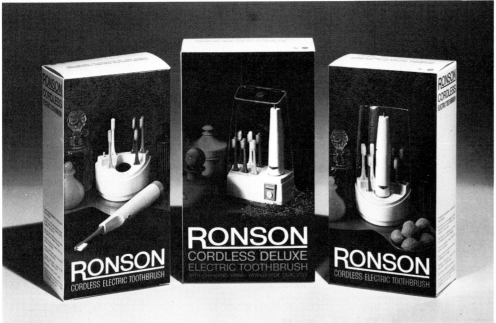

Among the benefits of certain point-of-purchase pieces are the demands created for them by the consumer. The souvenir collector of ashtrays, matchboxes, and the like receives as a by-product the advertiser's message. When the point-of-purchase piece is sufficiently sought after as a collector's item, the advertiser is indeed in an enviable position. Such is the case with the Löwenbräu Beer Mugs. They are shown displayed in their expanded polystyrene packer. The blind-embossed brand mark on the container was an added touch on what is disposable packing material.

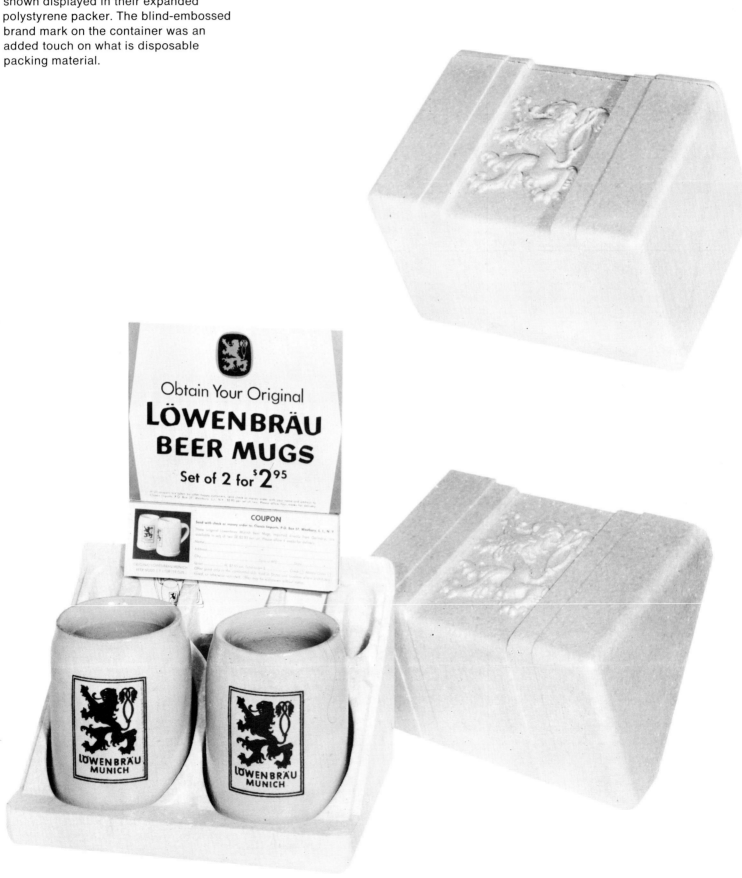

The Royal Ultronic Electric Typewriter corrugated carrying case is well designed in terms of graphics and construction. The carton can be opened and closed without string, tape, or wrapping paper, and can be carried with the plastic carrying handle which locks the top flap when the typewriter is being transported. It is printed in two colors, and a third color is achieved with the use of a colored handle.

The Ampex Stereo Headphones are protected, transported, and displayed in this carton. The rear panel, with the product description, folds down, and the entire display unit fits into the outer carton when the product is shipped or carried home by the consumer.

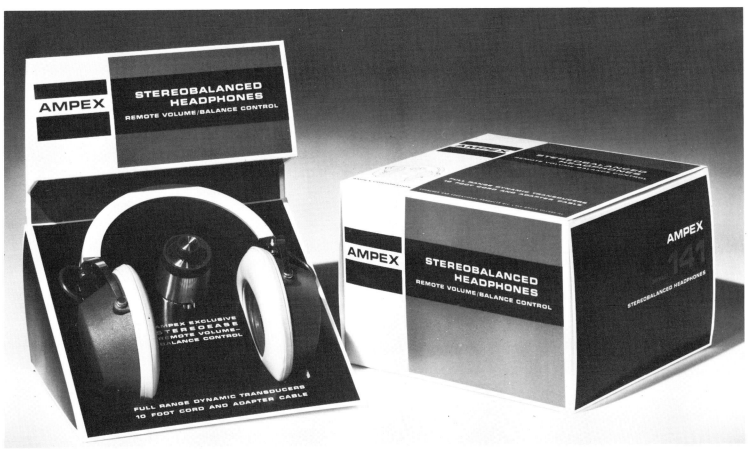

Often, the point of purchase is the consumer's doorstep. Buying Girl Scout Cookies leaves a charitable feeling in the mind of the purchaser, and these new cartons are a beautiful reminder. The carton for each type of cookie has a different photographic cover.

The Ames line of measuring instruments is graphically represented with a strong symbol and typography. Its display value in cluttered hardware stores is readily apparent.

The Tucker Marker is an ordinary folding carton turned into a four-sided display fixture that holds forty-eight marking pens. The dealer merely removes the outer packing and the pre-packed carton is ready for display.

The record-album cover and book dust jacket are vital point-of-purchase vehicles. The surfaces of each are cornucopias of graphic design: art, photography, typography, and all else that is graphics. Arbitrarily, I have chosen to illustrate a few examples of the record album that reflect various design solutions.

SING TO THE LORD
15 EARLY AMERICAN FOLK HYMNS
THE ROBERT SHAW CHORALE
ROBERT SHAW, CONDUCTOR

RCA VICTOR
RED SEAL

LM-2942

GALE GARNETT SINGS ABOUT FLYING & RAINBOWS & LOVE & OTHER GROOVY THINGS

RCA VICTOR
DYNAGROOVE
RECORDING

Don't Hurt Him
I Make Him Fly
Over the Rainbow
This Child
Look Who's Here
No Other Name
The Sun Is Gray
You're Doing Me
No Good
Just Wait and See
I Am Shining
You're Gone Now
Lie to Me Easy

LPM-3747

Delightful to give and to receive, these Joseph Magnin Company holiday gift boxes are constant reminders of the company beyond the point of sale. The value of advertising and good will generated by creative gift cartons is far in excess of cost, since the desire to have a collection of the various cartons may well result in multiple sales.

The Hathaway Shirt Company carton projects the famous eye patch in photography as well as graphics. It is an appropriately masculine gift box, with a contemporary look.

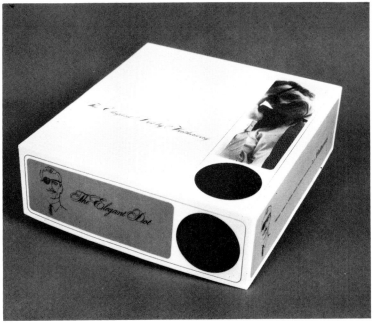

This Utica Club Trolley souvenir is distributed to visitors to the Utica Club Brewery—a happy give-away.

A "bottle topper" is usually a small cardboard display designed to circle the neck of a bottle and carry an advertising message. Thus a single bottle displayed with a bottle-topper message becomes its own display. The Calvert bottle toppers are more elaborate, but fall within this definition. They are colorful, typographically interesting, and individually shaped, and are an outstanding example of what designers can do with small space.

The White Satin Gin bottle carries the same message found on the cut-case display. The graphics are equally strong in the smaller size.

WINDOWS

The store window is valuable space from which the advertiser can reach the consumer. For the retailer, the window is an extension of his selling floor to the exterior. A message that registers at this level invites immediate sales—the only advertising message with a shorter distance between advertiser and consumer is the point-of-purchase display itself.

The utilization of the window, the space provided, and the materials needed vary with each industry. Some of the problems immediate to the design of a window are: the kind of store, the season in which the display will be used, the theme of national or promotional advertising, the nature of the product itself, and the manner of installation. The solution to each of these problems obviously affects the nature of the design, making it difficult to generalize about the problems. For example, the liquor store window, unlike the drugstore window, is subject to state and local ordinances throughout the country. The designer must therefore consider the restrictions on this industry.

What might be a common denominator is the need for flexibility. Window sizes vary; some are wide, some narrow; some have a see-through view into the store, others do not. The designer must consider all these factors and create a design that will not suffer in a small area or fall apart in a larger space. The unit must be easy to assemble, particularly if the retailer is to install it himself. While some advertisers provide their own window trim group to install their windows and others hire outside services, many depend upon the retailer. Whatever the method, the display should be functional and easy to set up.

Graphically, the problem is equally complex. But again there is a common denominator: the need for the window to project an instantly discernible message, a poster-like impact. Again this is dependent upon the store, because some windows, such as camera- and bookstore windows, invite window-shopping by their very organized clutter of merchandise.

While we are concerned with material that functions as its own backdrop for merchandise featured in the window, other advertising items are used in windows as well: paper streamers, banners, decals, signs, mounted posters, counter cards, and products.

The window display that is specifically created for a retail store by the store's own display department is an aspect of window design I will not cover. Certainly, some of the finest designs are being created by and for the use of department stores. Amazingly current, quick to change, retaining interest and consumer attention, they are indeed a continual source of inspiration for all designers. And, of course, it is always a treat to watch store windows during the Christmas season. But, although the store window is a point-of-purchase expression, we are concerned only about those materials prepared for store use by the advertiser.

The Helena Rubinstein window display is an example of advertising continuity at the point of purchase—the colorful drugstore window and the in-store merchandise display are both a visual extension of the original national advertising campaign. In the window display, the girl and the tulip are die-cut, and tab into the back card. The tulips in front of the girl are also die-cut to create another plane. The entire unit plus the two boxed tulips fold flat for shipping. The tulip window, while multi-planed, is simple to set up, requiring only the locking of easels and the insertion of a few tabs.

The two Dorothy Gray windows effectively use illustration to evoke different moods for their annual summer cologne promotion. Both units are excellent examples of shape that are die-cut to create flowing lines that reinforce the illustration. The construction and illustration are designed and function as one coordinated unit. These units fold easily and are quickly assembled.

The Imprévu window utilizes an exciting photograph from the Imprévu national advertising campaign. The design and basic construction of the center piece are a reiteration of the arch design on the Imprévu package. The die-cut picture of the bottle, strategically placed, is well photographed—the flat surface looks three-dimensional because of the camera angle and lighting. The window captures the freshness and excitement that are suggested by Imprévu usage.

The elaborate Marcel Rochas display is composed of many materials to achieve its rich, elegant look. The red background is flocked paper; the front plane is white velour. The figures and cartouche are gold-plated, vacuum-formed plastic. This unit is an example of a design making use of rich display materials to achieve its visual effect. The creative and effective use of these materials is no small undertaking for the designer. They must be applied with taste and restraint, and executed with knowledge. Most drugstore windows of this style are designed to be installed professionally.

The Chanel unit is a classic window that reflects, through design, the quality of the product line and its brand image. A simple stepped unit and shadow box are the basic construction elements. The use of ruled borders, the logo, and the sparse copy all work to unify the window and contribute to its classic feeling. This display window is a recognized symbol of Chanel.

The Helena Rubinstein units advertise make-up and face cream with different approaches in both graphics and construction. The Lightworks letters are partially die-cut and project in front of the background. The Gothic letters are the logo for this line of cosmetics. The polka-dot-patterned background is picked up from the packaging. The formal look of the Ultra Feminine unit is in keeping with the product image of the face cream. The three panels project forward from their center background.

All of these drugstore units have back panels that were used behind the main display. In addition to being decorative, the panels function as a control of the store window in several ways. First, they block the ability to see into the store. Secondly, they cover exposed window framing or any other structural unsightliness. Finally, they can expand to accommodate wide windows or fold for use in small areas.

Kodak provides the dealer with many items for use in camera-store windows, an important selling space. Shown are an aluminum frame with wire easel and shelf supports. The shelves are constructed of hardboard, and finished in various colors with silk-screened Kodak identification. The full-color lithographed panel is one of several that are distributed automatically to dealers during the year.

The Ladybird factory display humorously shows the manufacturing process of this producer of children's clothing. It was designed to be a centerpiece display for large department stores and smaller retail outlets throughout Britain. In large department stores, the unit was installed and trimmed by Ladybird's own merchandising force. The Fairy House was a natural theme to attract the attention of passing families, children in particular. The motion of the cartoon figures in each room is accomplished with oscillating motors.

The Sandtex and Snowcem lines of the Cement Marketing Company utilize the same basic display construction and were planned to be used in conjunction. The use of different but similar graphics makes each unit individual and yet related; the utilization of the same construction is economical.

A very playful and decorative window is the Candy Cupboard display. Note the motion of the side Santa units. The front flaps of these small units provide space for display of the product.

The Martin Senour window card presents a color chart in a simple construction. The color swatches are various shapes, adding to the charm of the chart and demonstrating how the simplest demand (in this case, for a color swatch) can be made interesting in the hands of creative designers. The display is particularly effective when shown among paint cans, brushes, and related items.

MARTIN SENOUR PAINTS

SHELTER TONES

Flat and gloss exterior finishes for every wood and masonry surface...for all climates.

pebble and sand

Colors to match and blend stone, concrete, stucco ... low-key color foils for natural or weathered wood.

town and country

Sophisticated deep body colors for restoring the brownstone town house or the sprawling Victorian...Sparkle with white trim.

painted desert

Catch the mood of the canyon country with colors to blend with stone, brick and all natural woods.

pale tints

...to lend size and story book charm to the small house...frost with white trim.

cool lagoon

Trim colors to echo the vibrating blues and greens of a sunlit seashore or inland lake.

Unlike other national advertisers, liquor companies can not distribute window displays to all national markets, because regulations covering liquor store window displays vary within each state and city. Therefore, promotions developed by the liquor companies are presented at national sales meetings to district sales managers, who select those materials applicable for use in their areas.

The Seagrams Summer Whiskey display is light in approach. The brand symbol is so familiar to the consumer that the design did not require illustration of the product. The fruits, which suggest mixed drinks, are made of vacuum-formed plastic.

The Calvert mobile is activated by a rotary electric motor. The brightly colored mobile is offset by the gold-foil background and rich brown panels.

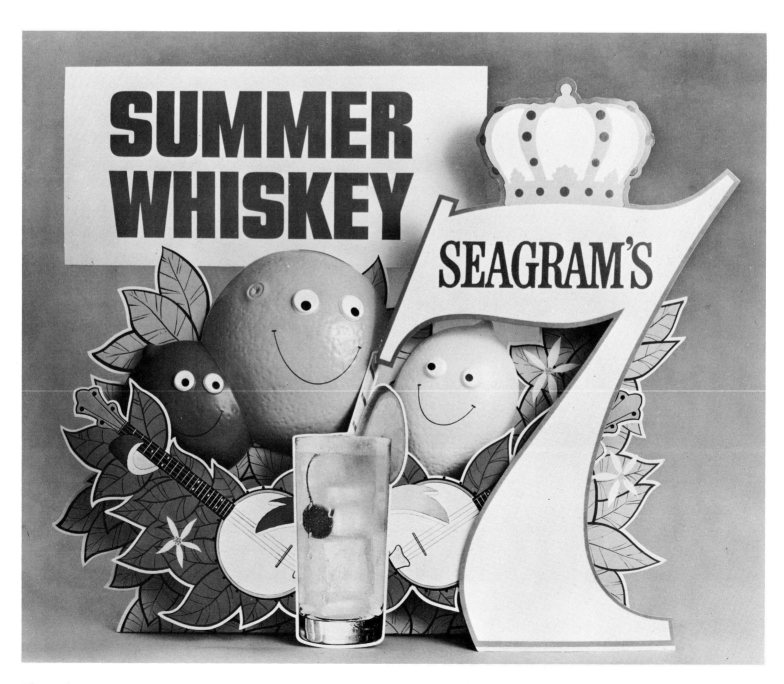

94

The great travel boom and the consequent need for travel-agent service have opened yet another market for point-of-purchase display design. The agent's premises and window are ideal environments for point-of-purchase displays to excite the mood of travel. Unlike supermarket and drugstore displays, travel advertisements lack a product but sell instead a concept, opening the way for design solutions free of merchandising problems.

The Aeronaves de Mexico window captures photographically the richness of ancient Mexico. The gold-colored metal mask is an authentic-looking touch that adds to the flavor of the unit, and it will long be part of the decor of the agent's premises.

The El Al blocks can stack decoratively in the window or on a counter, or be used in conjunction with other El Al display material. The boxes fold flat for easy shipment and assembly.

The camel, five and a half feet long, is a charming El Al travel piece. Printed on both sides, the cardboard unit ships flat and is assembled by the agent. It can serve as a window piece or as a floor-stand merchandiser, utilizing very little space. The use of the boxes with the camel crates an excellent window combining delightful whimsey and the realism of the photographic illustrations.

POSTERS

When utilized on billboards and other commercial space, the poster is an expression that does not fall within our definition of point-of-purchase. But the direct graphic statement, highly developed in this vehicle, is applicable to point-of-purchase design, and much can be learned from it.

In point-of-purchase, the poster is used in the store or store window. Supplied free to the dealer, it usually announces a promotion or product. It can be printed on paper, plastic, and cloth (banner), and is also called a streamer.

The importance of the paper poster used in the store window cannot be overemphasized. Some simple arithmetic will illustrate the value of this unmeasurable medium. Let us say ten thousand stores display our streamer. If a hundred people note the poster in a store window, then a total of a million people per day are exposed to a message that has cost the advertiser pennies to supply. (Paper posters are often printed with material used on the display, thereby getting a "free ride," with little production cost.)

However short the life of the poster, the value is far in excess of cost. If the message is strong enough, and presented in a way that easily communicates its message, some of the passers-by hopefully will enter the store and become consumers.

This Polaroid poster states the message clearly and succinctly in the tradition of poster graphics. Where pricing is a factor, pressure-sensitive numbers are supplied so that the dealer may add his price without destroying the layout. Pressure-sensitive tape is often added to the back of paper streamers as well. The dealer just removes the protective backing and hangs the poster.

The Pepsi poster is fresh, exciting, and directly related to the company's advertising theme. The ability to provide in-store promotional material directly related to national advertising, for maximum consumer exposure, is a point-of-purchase objective. The poster for L & M Menthol Tall is a similar example, particularly since this theme was used to introduce a new brand of cigarettes. Fresca was introduced with a "blizzard" advertising campaign, and the poster captures this feeling with freshness and zest.

The crisp keen taste.

The crisp keen taste of the Northland. New L&M Menthol Tall. 100 millimeters tall.

Taller than king size.

Taste that beats the others cold!

PEPSI·COLA

Frosty, refreshing, sugar free

FRESCA

TRADE-MARK ®

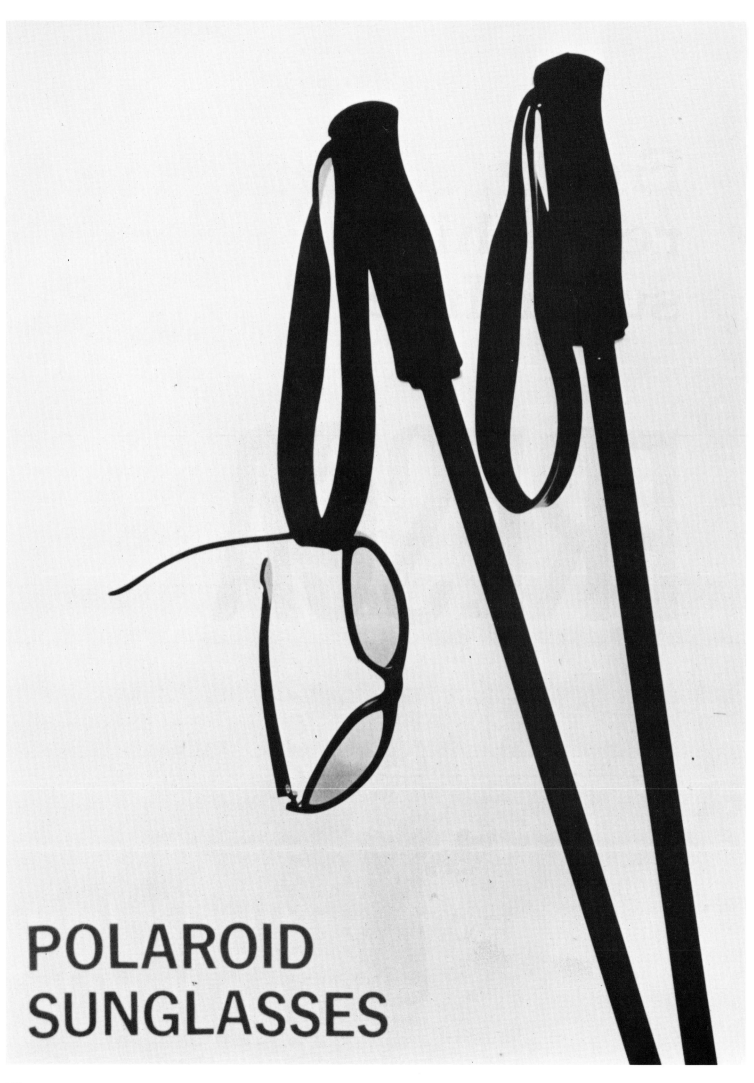

**POLAROID
SUNGLASSES**

This Polaroid poster used in Europe is notable for its clear statement of a message through the impact of a well-portrayed symbol.

The Eastern Airlines posters are representative examples of the company's clean, crisp style of communication. They are used by travel agents, both in windows and on walls, and very likely in the dens of favored customers. The directness of this approach is hard to surpass and must rank as classic in this field.

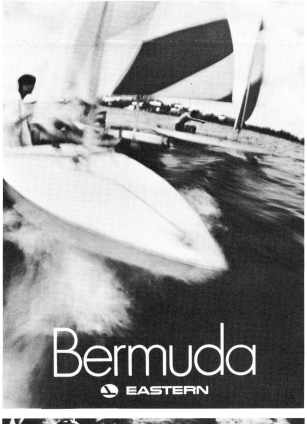

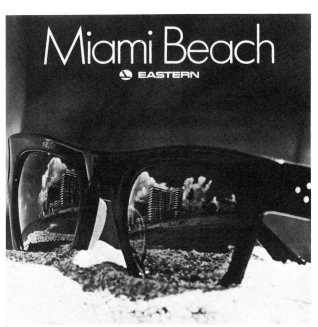

A poster mounted to paperboard and displayed by standing it on a counter or in a window is referred to as a "counter card." To support it, a paperboard easel is affixed to the center of the card and simply opens at a right angle to the card. The counter card serves a function similar to that of the poster, but has greater longevity. Often it is displayed near merchandise or has merchandise placed in front of it. The Schaefer poster is an example of a counter card.

The Ford clear acetate see-through poster has the advantage of not blocking the view from the street into the car showroom.

The various expressions of point-of-purchase are continually overlapping. When we speak of posters, particularly as used in windows, we must mention the decal (short for decalcomania). Generally printed on plastic or specially treated paper, it is used on windows, doors, products themselves, or any other smooth surface. Easiest to affix are the pressure-sensitive decals, though water immersibles are used as well. The decal and the transparent poster serve the same purpose. Their value is their see-through quality; they do not completely block a window, as can be seen from the example of the Polaroid color film message, printed on acetate.

Satin banners are available for each car in the Ford line. They are held wrinkle free by heavy chrome moldings at top and bottom.

An ego-pleasing tongue-in-cheek portrait of a travel agent was sent out by El Al to agents. Specific in appeal, its use was immediate and enthusiastic. El Al thereby became the recipient of much exposure. The banner is colorfully silkscreened on plasticized canvas.

HOMO SAPIENS PRAEPARATOR ITINERI
or (The Anatomy of a Travel Agent)

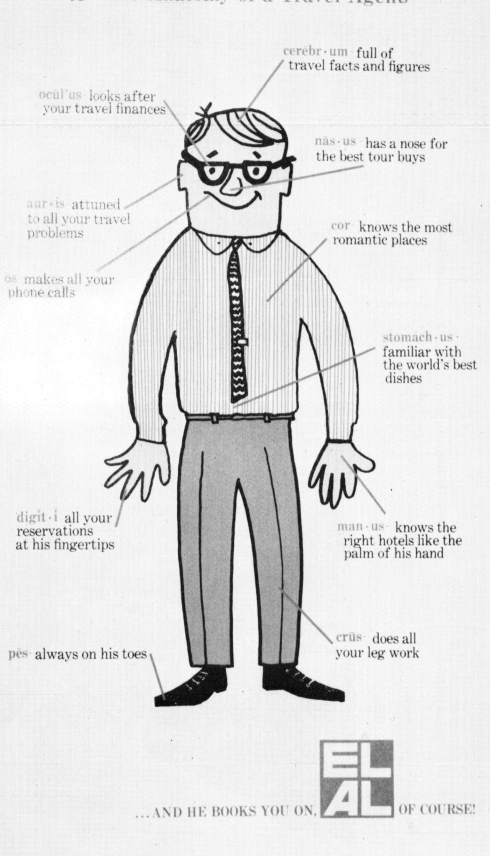

cerebr·um full of travel facts and figures

ocŭl'us looks after your travel finances

năs·us has a nose for the best tour buys

aur·is attuned to all your travel problems

cor knows the most romantic places

ōs makes all your phone calls

stomach·us familiar with the world's best dishes

digit·i all your reservations at his fingertips

man·us knows the right hotels like the palm of his hand

crūs does all your leg work

pēs always on his toes

...AND HE BOOKS YOU ON, **EL AL** OF COURSE!

Can you merchandise the cultural qualities of a city in much the same way—by building its image through smart design? In the Chicago poster program, civic graphics were created to inform and inspire the citizen about his city's diverse cultural activities and amusements. The posters are displayed throughout the city on aluminum stands which hold two posters back to back. Initiated, produced, and maintained voluntarily by private corporations and individuals, the program is under the aegis of the Committee for Cultural Communications; Chicago designer John Massey, the head of the committee, created the entire program.

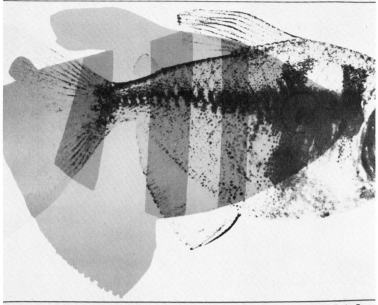

Shedd Aquarium

Lake front at Roosevelt Road, daily to 5 pm

chicago
has two great
zoos

lincoln park

run jump play look walk think dream

is the first letter of the alphabet
there are twenty-five more
the chicago public library has all of them
in some very interesting combinations

The poster is a powerful medium for marketing ideas as well as merchandise. The most famous poster ever produced in the United States must be James Montgomery Flagg's "Uncle Sam." First used in the era before mass magazines and radio, not to mention television, this poster and later ones mobilized the mind and spirit of America. The Uncle Sam poster itself was reissued in World War II and used in subsequent recruitment drives; its impact and emotion appeal for patriotic action have not lessened.

Victory is a Question of Stamina
Send—the Wheat
Meat·Fats·Sugar
the fuel for Fighters
UNITED STATES FOOD ADMINISTRATION

Will you have a part in Victory?

WRITE TO THE NATIONAL WAR GARDEN COMMISSION ~ WASHINGTON, D.C. for free books on gardening, canning & drying.

"Every Garden a Munition Plant"

BILL GRAHAM PRESENTS IN SAN FRANCISCO

DANCE   CONCERT

BUTTERFIELD BLUES BAND
JEFFERSON AIRPLANE
BIG MAMA MAE THORNTON

FILLMORE
AUDITORIUM

ADVANCE TICKETS   AT THE DOOR
$3.00 $3.50

TICKET OUTLETS

SAN FRANCISCO: City Lights Bookstore; The Psychedelic Shop; Bally Lo (Union Square);
The Town Squire (1318 Polk); S. F. State College; BERKELEY: Campus Records, Discount
Records; Shakespeare & Co. MILL VALLEY: The Mod Hatter SAUSALITO: The Tides Bookstore;
Rexall Pharmacy MENLO PARK: Kepler's Bookstore.

These "readable unreadables" use color, type, and illustrations in a unique manner (the roots of which are in psychedelic art) that is the antithesis of design "standards." Colors that clash, type that is difficult to read, and other aspects of "wrong" design become the positive appeal of these posters. Their success nullifies rules and rule-makers in design.

It must be remembered that the good, clear style that comes out of the "Bauhaus" tradition is a style in itself, and not the ultimate standard by which all design is to be measured. The designer can never be content with one format or one design system; he must not close his eyes to other possibilities.

SIGNS

As a point-of-sale device, the sign identifies companies and products, and may carry an advertising or informational message. A sign may be an integral part of a display, but, as commonly used, refers to a separate entity.

The entire field of signage is of increasing importance to the advertiser. The concern of corporations with their images and the projection of those images have resulted in a great improvement in signage. We constantly see the value of total corporate design in the market place. Quick identification and consistency of image are of vital importance in our highly mobile life. It is not by chance that the leading companies in industry have been among the first to employ signage as another marketing tool.

The designer concerned with the corporate logo is concerned with the same elements that are basic to all effective sign design. Indeed, it is in the medium of signage that a designer's effectiveness as a communicator is put to the test, because he has to make his statement with a minimum of means.

My examples show both interior and exterior signs designed to function at or near the point of sale. This material relates to mass-produced signs and omits both the custom sign, produced for individual use, and signage in architectural design.

It is not by accident that the Coca-Cola symbol is the most recognizable logo in the world. The history of Coca-Cola advertising, particularly signage, is the classic example of the successful utilization of the point-of-purchase medium. From the very beginning of Coca-Cola's history, there is no place that some Coca-Cola sign has not appeared. It would be a welcome sign to astronauts landing on the moon. (And it would be there, if Coca-Cola felt so inclined!)

The Coca-Cola logo has been used on every conceivable point-of-purchase advertising vehicle and, where none existed, Coca-Cola created one. Thus we see the red circle and the famous script on everything from Tiffany lamps to paper cups and plastic signs.

The successful use of the logo has not gone unchanged. Never content with success, the company continually improves and updates its identification program. Added to it have been "Coke" signs, "things go better with Coke" typography, and, most recently, the "floating star" design developed for illuminated signs. The contemporary sign with the floating-star pattern is one of the latest uses of the famous Coca-Cola script. It was not an easy problem to create a new sign that would be different and contemporary, and yet retain the familiar look of Coca-Cola signage. Every possible problem had to be thoroughly evaluated, in order to achieve maximum success.

The unit consists of three panels arranged to form an exact square. The top panel bears the famous Coca-Cola logotype. The lower panel bears the dealer's name or message. (A personalized sign insures long usage.) The center panel is designed with ten embossed oval domes, made of plexiglass that permits an unusual see-through effect. Behind the domes are three-dimensional, translucent plastic "stars" arranged in an alternate color pattern of aquamarine and lime green, colors compatible with the red background of the trademark. The choice of these colors was the result of much experimentation, including the creation of a color wheel designed around Coca-Cola red. Light is reflected downward and upward from fluorescent lamps in the upper and lower panels, creating a sparkling effect. The star shapes are structured alternately in a convex-concave arrangement, so that the overall lighting is smooth, with equal intensity of light on either side of the sign. The center panel of floating stars separates the logo from the dealer message yet acts as unifying element, enhancing the look of the total sign.

Coca-Cola's success has been achieved by other leading companies who, in their own way, have used point-of-purchase constantly to remind the consumer of their products.

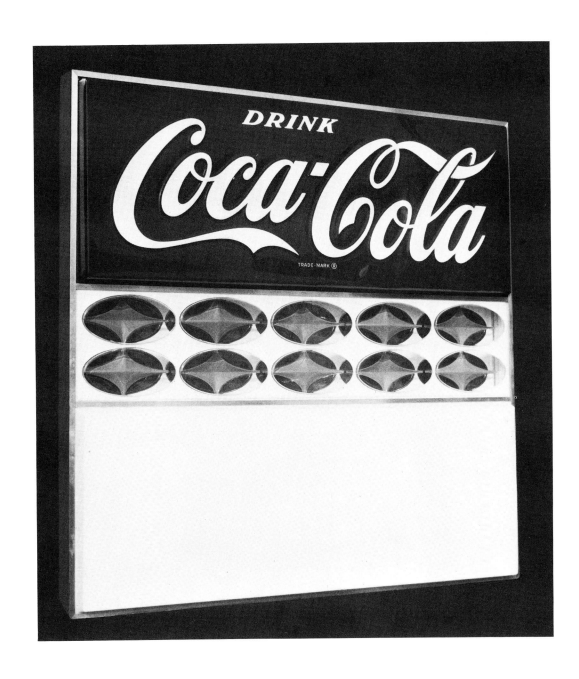

Another giant of American industry with a recognizable logo that has been effectively utilized in point-of-purchase is Kodak. The yellow film box, shown here in a heavy-gauge metal replica, and the logo both contribute to its instant identification. Both the box and the outdoor metal hanging sign have a baked enamel finish in Kodak yellow, red, and black.

The Mobil sign is the result of a total corporate design program that researched and evaluated all their graphics. The study included the design and recognition of service stations, as well as packaging and signage. One result that we can illustrate is the logo and shape of signs used in Mobil stations. The small o is in red; the other letters are in blue. This seemingly restrained use of color is a unique identifier. The result is a bold, crisp, and contemporary solution, easily visible both day and night. A strong trademark, the Mobil logo is equally successful on a letterhead and on a five-foot illuminated sign.

Red and blue with black type, often framed with a yellow border, the Pepsi sign is graphically strong, and is unquestionably its own message.

Those companies who have the good fortune to have logos that are recognizable have been equally fortunate in not changing them throughout the years. At this time, with so much emphasis on corporate redesign, not only are corporate names represented by initials and symbols, but they have become look-alikes and unmemorable images. This has been a flagrant violation of the designer's responsibility to communicate. One need only study the Ford sign program to see a modern look coupled with the memorable Ford script. The designer has a responsibility to history as well as to the future.

Graphics must bear a relationship to the product; it must project the inherent being of that which it identifies. It should not reflect the designer's nature but his interpretation of the problem. Not every corporation is an I.B.M., and therefore the corporate design must reflect its unique corporate identity. One could not conceive of replacing the Coca-Cola, Kodak, Ford, or Goodyear logo to fit "today's" design thinking. As a matter of truth, these marks have survived the design look of the twenties, thirties, forties, fifties, and sixties; they did not change with every new style. The list is longer than the graphic community would care to admit. Today's problem in packaging is to create a package that will yield the recognition of a Coca-Cola or a Kodak product. It cannot happen with look-alike design solutions.

The creation of a corporate mark is an exciting challenge for the designer. The opportunity to symbolize the image of a company through abstraction and/or typography is a graphic problem of the highest order. The assumption must be made that the designer will accept the challenge in terms not only of the visual conception of a corporate mark but also in its application, for it is the manifold uses of the symbol that will be the measure of its success.

The implementation of just one aspect of such a problem can be illustrated by the Ford Dealership Identity Program.

Awesome in the magnitude of the project, its successful development and implementation on a national level is a credit to the Ford corporate design group. To begin a program of creating signs for their dealership required a complete study of what such a sign should do, why, and how. Answers to questions of this nature do not come from sitting at a board; obviously this information must be researched both from Ford's own dealers and from sign-industry sources.

Simply stated, it was necessary to develop a sign program that would be visually consistent throughout the country, so that Ford dealers could be identified in any state. Secondly, the sign had to state the brand of vehicle sold by the dealer.

One of the problems Ford did not have was the need to create a new logo. The script Ford, used in an oval, is their corporate symbol, second only to Coca-Cola in consumer recognition. That the script represented the parent company, and not the brand, was a problem that had to be solved visually so that the consumer would know which dealership the sign represented. It was solved by dividing the names on the sign and by the use of color. The Ford script, the symbol of the parent company, would always be in a deep blue (Corporate Blue), the Ford division in a lighter blue (Ford Blue), Mercury in a rich burgundy (Mercury Red), Lincoln in black (Lincoln Black), and the truck division in a bright vermilion (Truck Red).

The sign grows out of a tapered, anodized, brushed-aluminum escutcheon in a flowing manner. The pole meets the sign at the point of division between brand and corporate names. Supporting signs (leasing, service, used cars, etc.) were developed with equal attention to their use with the brand signs. In addition, suggested dealerships, signs, and facia brands were created. The concern was with the dealership's total environment, and the total effect is automotive in its clean, crisp lines.

Trucks are a corporate product and therefore do not need a divisional brand name. The impact of the sign can be seen in the photograph of it in use. Note the clarity of the graphics when the sign is correctly scaled to the site: it is large and, when placed on the hill, overshadows the other sign in the picture.

Used-car lots sell all makes of automobiles; consequently used-car signs do not require the corporate mark. In all other ways, they are designed exactly like the brand signs, for continuity of image.

Shown is a Lincoln Mercury brand sign in use. Note the service sign next to the main sign; all supporting signs were color-matched to the brand sign.

The dealership identity program includes recommendations for use and materials available to the dealer for his own name sign. They are illuminated or non-illuminated, in individual letters or full panels. To add to the completeness and continuity of all signage, facia bands are recommended for use along the entire building. The dealer signs are in the same color as the brand sign, and when all the materials are used together, the results are distinctive.

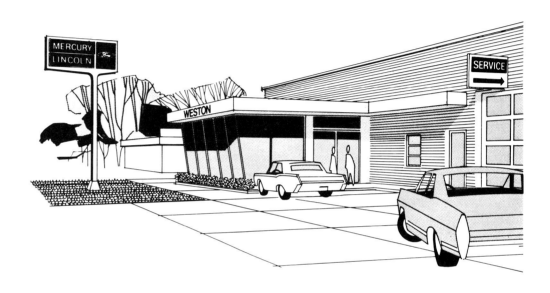

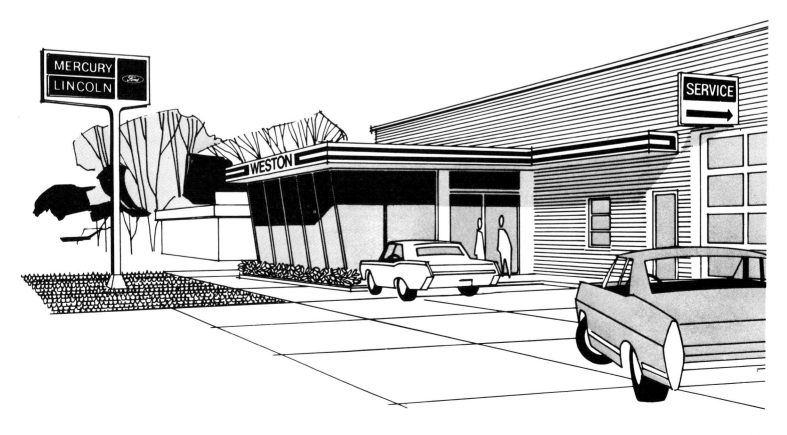

Discover America Inc. was formed in 1965 as private industry's response to a Congressional resolution and Presidential proclamation which urged the development of a program to stimulate greater travel in this country. Traveling in the United States and its territories would be encouraged for Americans and citizens of foreign lands, to discover and enjoy the scenic, historical, cultural, educational, recreational, and industrial attractions of our nation.

Thus the United States became a merchandising problem. Through advertising and promotion with leading companies, it has indeed been successfully marketed. No small measure of its success is its logo. The Discover America logo is an outstanding design, incorporating all of the attributes of a successful logo. For one, the weather vane is an excellent symbol suggesting farms and the basic roots of America. The stars and colors (red, white, and blue) add to this feeling. The arrow suggests direction and, thereby, travel. And, all important, it states its purpose —Discover America—within its design. The entire unit clearly fulfills its objectives.

The Pearl Brewery Company's entry into the on-tap market required the creation of point-of-purchase material with a unique look. Its appeal had to satisfy the retailer, so that the material would be used, and the consumer, so that the product would be requested. The various materials had to be harmonious when used together, yet flexible enough to stand alone, to fit individual dealers' needs.

The featured unit is a canopy and revolving centerpiece, around which the entire Pearl point-of-purchase program was designed. The arching canopy, made of permanent fiber glass with genuine walnut inserts, easily attaches overhead; the revolving centerpiece is suspended from it. On one side is a clock, the Pearl Logo, and "On Tap" in raised gold letters. On the other side are stylized beer glasses in yellow-stained glass against a background of amber bottle glass; the logo and "On Tap" are repeated. The entire unit is encased in a walnut housing, and, if desired, can be used without the canopy. Note the tiny spotlights in the two outside canopies; they highlight the serving area.

The illuminated cash register sign utilizes the same visual elements of the program.

DISCOVER AMERICA

The introduction of a new product by an established company often requires the product to have its own brand image and identification, different not only from the well-known brands of the parent company, in this case Budweiser, but also from all other competitive products. To accomplish this, one of the most unusual sign units for promoting beer (or any product) was designed and produced. It is particularly interesting to note the technical considerations of this spherical unit. It is a five-foot rotating sphere with three sign facings, each protected from the weather by plexiglass bubbles. Each section is hinged so that individual panels can be changed when necessary. The lamp and motor, both located inside the unit, are accessible through the panels. This arrangement is unique for outdoor signs and eliminates the bulky outdoor motion box usually used. The spheres show the logo, the product, and the name of the tavern quite clearly. Thus, the Busch sign is effective in its technical solutions as well as its design.

The Busch spheres are reinterpreted in this small cash register sign. The spheres revolve, revealing logo, transparency (changeable to suit the location of the unit), and clock.

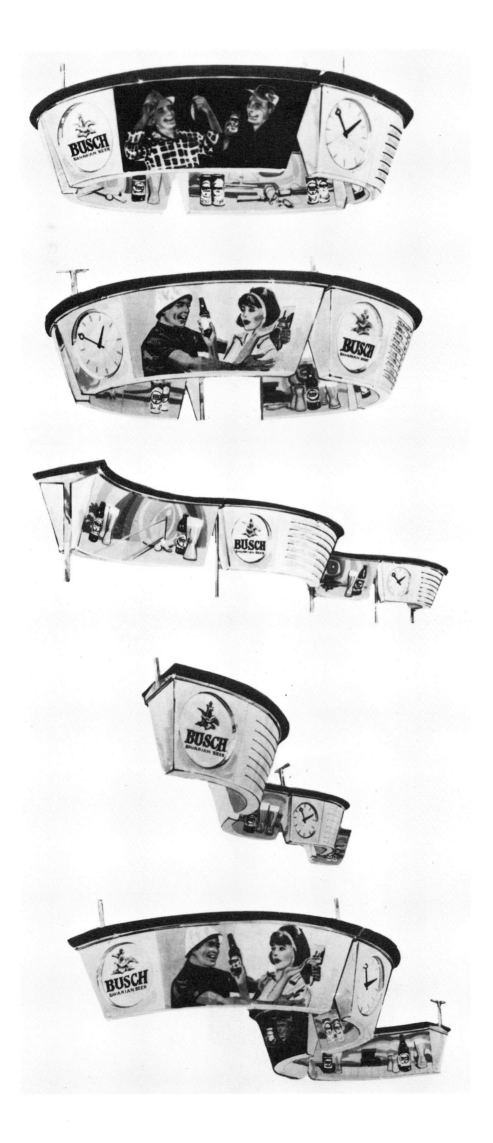

The competition for display space is even more critical inside taverns, particularly when there are point-of-purchase materials already provided by established manufacturers. It was therefore decided to find an area in the tavern not already heavily dominated by competition—hence, the creation of an overhead unit of tremendous flexibility and variety of application. The double-faced sign can be used as a continuous serpentine, a semicircle, or a complete circle. By using different transparencies, it was further individualized, so that scenes of local interest could be used in various locations. The same structure with interior changes, such as changeable price panels, and appealing transparencies, was provided to off-premises locations, thereby retaining a consistent image. The basic unit was one of the largest injection-molded pieces ever manufactured.

It is apparent from this unit as well as the outdoor sign that successful innovations in design originate from total involvement in and understanding of marketing problems. To have made a sign similar in use and appearance to competing ones would not have been enough to aid this new product at the point of purchase.

The vacuum-formed ice tongs hold the Utica Club simulated carton. The unit is suspended from the ceiling in supermarkets, and is light enough to rotate slowly with natural air pressure. The four sides are printed in photogel.

The Schaefer stein is a good interpretation of a somewhat stock point-of-purchase problem, the visualization of animated bubbles. This unit uses a heat-activated bubbler and strategically located reflectors. The reflected bubbling animation and the illumination make this an especially realistic product display.

The current Coca-Cola lamp is a replica in synthetic materials of the now famous original Tiffany lamp.

Three wall plaques illustrate well the capacity of the manufacturers of point-of-sale signs to create both the old and the new with equal facility.

The Löwenbräu wall unit is vacuum-formed and antiqued with gold to simulate the texture of an old sign. The lion, the Löwenbräu symbol, is plated to look like metal.

The Fyfe & Drum sign is authentic looking from typography to worm holes. It is injection-molded of high-impact polystyrene; the fyfe and drum were molded separately and sprayed in eleven colors with the use of electro-formed spray masks. The drum sticks also were molded separately and attached to the top. The background was finished in antique green with black copy. The result is an authentic looking sign in thirteen colors, produced with modern materials, that duplicate the look of a hand-painted sign.

The Schmidt's herald is injection-molded of high-impact polystyrene. The entire plaque was gold-plated, sprayed, and hot-stamped in red and black. The technique of plating gives the unit its shiny metallic look. Two signs made of the same materials thus appear completely different because of the finishing technique used.

The Falstaff unit is a unique cash register sign that is both illuminated and animated. The shield is illuminated and the mugs clink in an animated pendulum motion. Mechanically, the same motor that runs the clock provides the energy necessary to activate the two toasting mugs. This is a well-conceived unit that combines utility (the clock), interest (clinking mugs), and family identity (Falstaff logo), all in one.

Wall clocks are point-of-purchase utility items of obvious value. Their creation is a challenge to the designer who seeks novel answers to problems. The Four Roses brand symbol is so well known that no copy need identify the origin of the clock.

The Coca-Cola clock is a handsome design that effectively uses the company's bright red logo. Perhaps a future collector's item like the original Tiffany lamp.

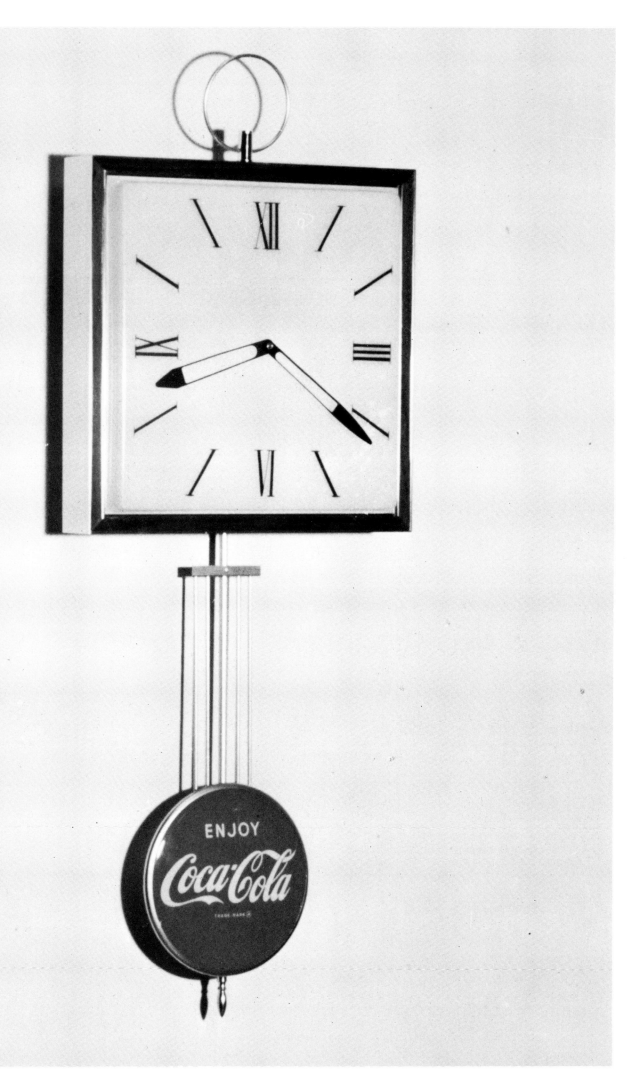

The Mattingly and Moore vacuum-
formed plastic sign is a delightful
"back-bar" identifier. Note the area at
left for price insertion.

Advertising at the point of purchase is
international in methodology. The Ger-
man Wine and Trade Association spon-
sored the Harlequin carnival promotion.
Materials prepared included the
vacuum-formed Harlequin sign shown
here, window posters, bottle toppers,
and wine cards.

Coca-Cola supplies this menu board
and these sign boards; the latter have
areas for the insertion of new photographs.

Service station point-of-purchase requirements are basically the same throughout the industry, because they have similar structures, space problems, and merchandising techniques. Thus, see-through clear plastic posters are used so that dealers' windows are not blocked. Most stations are far from the road, so headline lettering must be large and bold, and there is great use of fluorescent ink. Around the station are various places that require point-of-purchase displays of weatherproof materials and windproof constructions.

"Put a Tiger In Your Tank," the advertising message that found its way into the language of the country, was successfully communicated at the point of purchase. The promotion was well supported at the service station with many signs, tiger tail give-aways, and related promotional devices.

The following Humble material was produced at various times in support of the tiger promotion.

The Tiger pump topper was vacuum-formed of high-impact polystyrene and screened in five colors. It was manufactured in two pieces and assembled at the service station with clips that were provided, then fastened to the top of the gasoline pump by means of pressure-sensitive pads.

The light pole sign, approximately twenty-eight by eighteen inches, was silk-screened on outdoor corrugated board and held together with wing nuts; it was designed to attach to a light pole on the service station driveway, where it would have good exposure to driveway traffic.

This charging tiger sign, forty-two by eighty-four inches, was made of ribbed polyethelene and supported by wood slats on the top and bottom. Two signs were fastened back-to-back on the pole.

The button, long a device for election campaigns, sporting events, and conventions, has found new expression. Its use by the individual as a personal expression has become a national fad, particularly among young people. The wearer thereby becomes the medium of his own message. Quite naturally, advertisers have joined the craze with their own sales message. The "We try harder" Avis button captured the imagination of the public and is quite possibly the most successful advertising button ever produced. The button, as a give-away at the point of sale, is an excellent device for corporate advertising. Shown are some recent commercial and non-commercial examples.

The sign used to identify companies and products is our concern in point-of-purchase. The sign as an identifier of a street, highway, building, or station is beyond the definition of point-of-purchase, but is not beyond the concern of the designer. Those companies involved with total design are equally involved with signage, however it is used. Thus, C.B.S. designed special elevator numerals in keeping with all graphics in their great building. This is the case in many buildings of architectural achievement. It is equally so in exhibits that present graphic problems of signage for the designer to solve.

This is best illustrated by the sign program developed by Paul Arthur Associates for the Canadian Corporation for the 1967 World Exhibition (CCWE). At Expo 67, visitors found their way around the fairgrounds through a system of unified typography, pictograms, and color-coded signage. A standard sign manual was prepared that outlined the identification and information signs for which CCWE would be responsible. The individual exhibitors could relate their signage to this material, and all external signs by exhibitors had to be approved by CCWE. The manual was so detailed that it even included instructions on letter spacing. The basic CCWE sign was one of black lettering (Univers) on a white or natural mat aluminum background, with colored horizontal stripes to designate the four areas at Expo. (Each area was assigned a specific color.)

1.23 Caractères

L'échelle en bas sera utilisée comme guide pour l'espacement des lettres sur toutes les enseignes de la Compagnie Canadienne de l'Exposition Universelle. Il est recommandé que les exposants, les commanditaires et les concessionnaires l'emploient sur leurs propres enseignes lorsque le cas se présente. Les quatre espaces horizontaux, à la gauche du tableau indicateur, contiennent les caractères dont les positions ont déjà été établies. Le nombre d'unités entre le caractère fixe et le caractère suivant se trouve à l'opposé du caractère fixe, sous la colonne d'en-tête dans laquelle le caractère suivant apparaît. Une unité est 1/32" de la hauteur d'une majuscule. Donc, l'unité pour les séries E (hauteur des majuscules 2") des lettres de l'Expo est 1/16". L'espace entre les mots est de 18 unités (sauf après une ponctuation où l'espace est de 15 unités).

1.23 Letterform

The table below will be used as a guide in establishing inter-letter spacing on all CCWE signs, and it is urged that exhibitors, sponsors and concessionaires make use of it in their own signs, wherever applicable.
The four horizontal spaces on the left of the chart contain the characters whose positions have already been fixed. The number of units between the fixed character and the next is found opposite the column heading in which the next character occurs. One unit is 1/32 of the given cap. ht. Thus the unit for Expo letter series E, 2" cap. ht. is 1/16". The space between words is 18 units (except after punctuation where the space is 15 units).

	bhijklmnpru .,;:!-$&	acdegoqsz 2356890	fjtvwxy 147
GHIJMNU adghijlmnqu 1-!&$	6	5	4
BDEFORSZ bcefkopstz 356890	5	4	3
CKLPQX rvwxy 247	4	3	2
ATVWY	3	2	1

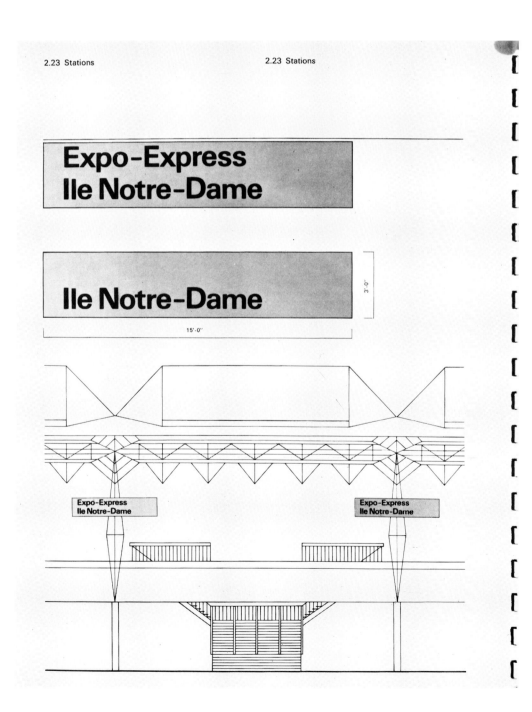

Because it was an international fair, pictographs were developed and used wherever possible; two examples are shown. The development of a basic pictorial symbol of world-wide understanding is a challenge to design. Major corporations, for example, are concerned with the need for international communication. Many efforts in this area have been made, and some, under the aegis of international representatives of business and industry, may soon realize a successful fruition. The need for universal symbols in our mini-world of jet travel and telstar is obvious.

Thus, Expo 67 was an example rich in opportunities for study in all aspects of design—design in its fullest definition. More specifically, the Expo signage relates directly to point-of-purchase problems. Certainly large shopping centers can benefit from unified signage; so can individual department stores. Many supermarkets and multi-departmental retail stores are completely without a coherent system of identification and information, but proper identification is necessary if merchandise is to be found and sold. Thus, the example of exhibit signage is not without practical application in point-of-purchase.

2.4 Pictogrammes

	Directions
1	Entrée
2	Sortie

	Interdictions
3	Feu interdit
4	Défense de toucher
5	Electricité
6	Entrée interdite
7	Défense de rester debout
8	Défense de s'asseoir
9	Propreté

	Renseignements et service d'urgence
10	Téléphone
11	Hôpital
12	Soins d'urgence
13	Objets trouvés
14	Invalides

	Désignation d'endroits
15	Toilettes—femmes
16	Toilettes—hommes
17	Restaurant
18	Café (buvette)

	Services de transport
19	Station d'autobus
20	Port de plaisance
21	Quai du bateau-passeur

	Autres services
22	Armoire-consigne
23	Vestiaire
24	Fournisseurs (entrée)

2.4 Pictographs

	Direction
1	Entrance
2	Exit

	Prohibition
3	No fire
4	Don't touch
5	Electricity
6	No admission
7	No standing
8	No sitting
9	Anti-littering

	Urgent information and service
10	Telephone
11	Hospital
12	First-aid
13	Lost-Found
14	Handicapped

	Room identification
15	Women's WC
16	Men's WC
17	Restaurant
18	Coffee Shop (refreshments)

	Transportation
19	Bus Station
20	Marina
21	Ferry Dock

	Other services
22	Locker
23	Cloakroom
24	Delivery (entrance)

SELLING ENVIRONMENTS
Vehicles

The itinerant peddler had his beginnings in man's earliest commercial activities. The covered wagon, filled with pots and pans, racing from town to town with Indians in pursuit, is part of our Western folklore in the United States and is, historically, the origin of some of our great department stores. The mobile vehicle, selling its own wares, is still much a part of our life. The truck bell signals Good Humor Ice Cream for young and old; the gong of the knife grinders can still be heard. There are mobile amusement rides, traveling libraries and art shows. In New York City, the tensions of crowded city life have been lessened by on-wheels jazz concerts and other live productions; traveling to underprivileged parts of the city, they bring music and imagination into these streets.

The growth of suburban areas, many far from city shopping centers, is filled with potential for new services and products. Certainly, the young mother busy with her family and isolated from the main would be receptive to a mobile store outside her home. Just what should be sold and could be sold must be determined. But the market place of the future may well be just beyond the driveway.

An excellent example of selling directly to the consumer has been the ice-cream vendor. The Good Humor truck, whether cycle-pushed or driven, has been a welcome sight for youngsters for many generations.

The latest example of mobile vending is the "soda fountain on wheels." The first mobile unit, Mr. Softee, took soft ice cream directly to the consumer. It was developed in Philadelphia in 1954; prior to that, the consumer had to drive to roadside stands for popular soft ice cream. Mr. Softee motorized vehicles are equipped to dispense ice cream, sundaes, milkshakes, and floats. With this innovation in merchandising, the founders of Mr. Softee created a new point-of-purchase mobile trade and the world's largest mobile soft ice cream organization.

Many communities today are serviced by home delivery of ready-to-serve snacks or dinners. This too is a change in the selling environment. But these are actually "deliveries" of merchandise previously prepared and ordered; the vehicle that delivers does not in itself generate sales. That it could is another innovation in marketing that perhaps will come in the future.

The development of new and revolutionary equipment is often difficult to explain in brochures. In such instances one demonstration is worth a thousand words. The "Typositor," a projection type machine that sets headlines and subheads to size, slants and proportions letters right in the machine, was a unique innovation in film lettering. The cost of the machine made its ownership practical for lithographers, typographers, printers, publishers, and art studios, as well as the graphic arts departments of manufacturing companies. The need therefore was to be able to reach those potential customers with a demonstration of the machine.

Thus the DemOvan, which brings the Typositor to the prospective buyer, was created. It is custom built and completely equipped for full-scale demonstrations, given in an environment of walnut paneling, carpeting, indirect lighting, airconditioning and heating, with custom settees and chairs. It has custom compartments for storing sales literature and carries its own power supply generator, insulated water tanks, and a vacuum cleaner. The rear compartment accommodates six complete Photo Typositors for immediate delivery, in addition to supplies, installation and maintenance equipment.

Shown is a recent service truck with the new corporate logo.

Visual Graphics Corporation

The Armour Abrasives Company has developed a "mobile" showroom to get its story directly to potential customers. "Innovator" is a sales tool that aids in developing markets throughout the United States, by reinforcing strong marketing areas and strengthening weak areas.

Thus, the itinerary of the Innovator is planned regionally, and each territory manager has an outline of his responsibilities, which start three weeks before the arirval of the unit and end with follow-up duties after the vehicle leaves his area. An invitation, with a cardboard dummy of the Innovator, is sent to prospective clients.

The ideal showing conditions would involve three customers per showing and three showings per day. The presentation is made by the sales promotion manager and lasts approximately fifteen minutes. The entire showing is automated, and includes slides, film, lights, music, a self-erecting three-dimensional display, and a two-dimensional electronically activated display. The full display area is seven feet by ten feet. The film and slides telling the Armour story are rear projection because of the limited space. In 1966, the Unit traveled 17,000 miles and was well received throughout the tour. Each year, new materials are developed for presentation.

Shown is the panel map of the United States with Armour facilities annotated. During the presentation, the map slides back into the wall, revealing the wall sculpture. The sculpture with moving parts is made with Armour products.

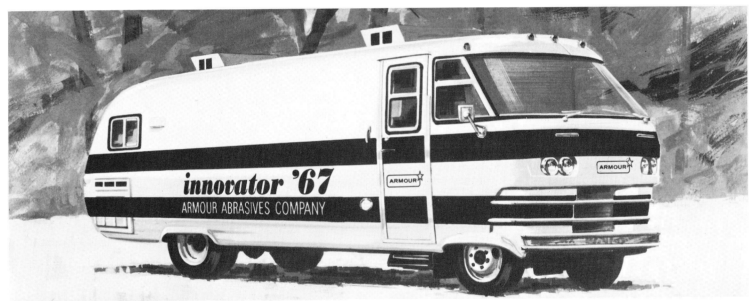

Environments

Point-of-purchase, as we have broadly defined it, involves many areas of graphics in the market place. The image of the product, we have often stated, must be consistent, from the package to signs to in-store promotion. The attitude of total concern for design need not stop at this point; the designer can control the in-store environment as well. Moreover, he should be concerned with the exterior of the store and the surroundings in which the store exists. In the shopping center, the civic center, and in all of town planning, there is room and need for design attitudes to be expressed and incorporated. No one can limit the scale of a designer's considerations; he can quest for his own star.

Certainly we have professed ambitions into other areas of professional endeavors, which may seem at first to be beyond our own ken. Architecture, town planning, and interior design are all highly specialized fields. And yet the graphic designer can function as an equal partner to help or even direct such a collaboration. Leading graphic designer Lou Dorfsman was responsible for every aspect of design in Eero Saarinen's C.B.S. building. Leading corporations are developing design centers that include teams of graphic and industrial designers, architects, and interior designers. The needs of today's corporations are manifold, and are best served by such collaborations.

Throughout this book, the designer has been reminded of his responsibility, to be concerned with all that is happening around him. Thus, in this survey of point-of-purchase we insist on the consideration of environments. Now let us speak of environments in terms that are meaningful to the advertiser—sales. Environment control is sales control.

Display merchandisers, as we have discussed them, are sold to the advertiser to move products. The growth of the display business and its future are predicated on the acceptance of this premise. Therefore, as more industries use displays and continue to market new products, we will find retail stores saturated with point-of-purchase materials. Supermarkets and drugstores already abound with merchandisers. For this reason we must be ready to discard the function of individual displays for newer ways of mass merchandising.

Perhaps the retailer will accept a total environment, developed by the advertiser, which will replace the many displays he receives; perhaps this environment will organize inventory and, through its uniqueness, sell more merchandise.

Hopefully, the impetus for and the creation of the point-of-purchase environment will come from increased marketing responsibilities undertaken by the point-of-purchase industry. It has been the history of this industry to meet the challenges of retailing and to initiate innovations within it.

Design in our time is fast-moving; innovations in the visual arts occur almost simultaneously and grow out of each other. Ideas are absorbed into the culture as quickly as they are developed. They are expanded upon or discarded with equal rapidity. The origins of mixed media can be traced to Moholy Nagy and his concepts of visual education and expression. His studies in painting, sculpture, film, and light kinetics have been synthesized into the expressions of today—the teachings of the twenties have become the vanguard of the sixties. Never again will there be such a time lag between theory and application.

In 1961-62, designer Ken Isaacs, working at the Illinois Institute of Technology, developed what he called an Informational Matrix, popularly referred to as "the knowledge box." A simple structure out of which came a gigantic concept, it is a completely closed, six-walled, lightless chamber made of masonite boards bolted to a wooden frame. Mounted outside of it are twenty-four slide projectors controlled by a central switch. By selection and programming of the slides, the environment inside the chamber can be controlled. The viewer is confronted with images on all four walls and on the floor and ceiling. The chamber becomes a new experience, a new reality. Conceived as a teaching device, it can communicate knowledge quickly and memorably. The projection of text, photographs, and light in a panoply of images is a memorable experience; the mind absorbs these events quickly and intelligently in a conceptual way. Any subject could be programmed for use in the box.

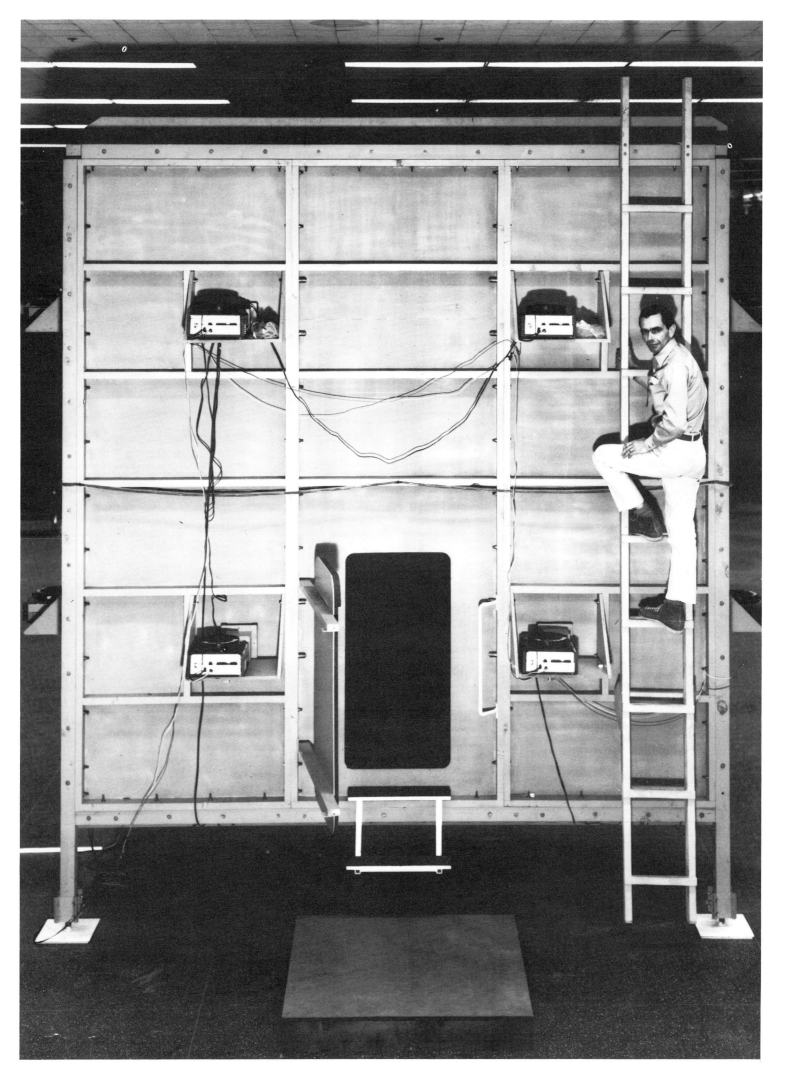

The photographs are of the original structure and initial programming experiment. Designer Ken Isaacs stands outside the Informational Matrix. Shown are some of the early trial programmings of the Matrix: text projected backward to test its effectiveness without concern for content, the head of a man projected onto all six surfaces, and the projection of multi-photographic images.

Just as the structure was created to rapidly expand knowledge, the principles of the machine itself have been rapidly adapted into our daily life. Its commercial counterpart has already been applied in discothèques and similarly planned commercial happenings, where lights, slides, and films all work together to affect the individual.

Shown flat, in scale to the figure, is the total informational area projected within the twelve-foot-square informational matrix. Each slide module is six feet square, a combination of four equaling one side of the six-sided cube. Therefore, the projection of this material would require a screen area twenty-four by thirty-six feet. Quite obviously, the impact of the six-sided projection would be lost; the informational Matrix shows all this material in a smaller area, and it is much more effective by surrounding the viewer from every direction.

The Cheetah, the "now club" where something different is going on all the time, is not a discothèque and not a night club in the traditional sense. Cheetah is the apogee of electronics, lights, slides, used in a total, ever changing environment. Three thousand colored bulbs, electronically controlled, change color with the music's intensity. Three bands rotate on the stage, which is an integral part of the dance floor. The environment is as flexible and ever changing as the people who attend. The club is a constant kaleidoscope of activity where no one event happens twice.

Its success since its opening in 1966 has led to Cheetah clubs being set up across the nation and abroad. The success of the original boutique at Cheetah has resulted in the development of a nation-wide chain of boutiques. They feature clothing, jewelry, accessories, and even home furnishings, many under the franchised Cheetah label.

The Cheetah concept successfully engaged the "under twenty-five" audience to which it was directed. Its innovations have influence beyond that audience into the "over twenty-five" world and into the very fabric of our society.

Fillmore Auditorium in San Francisco is yet another environment with its own inner life. Live music, slides, sound, dancing, and, above all else, the people melt into one being that becomes Fillmore. The result of this collective euphoria is the emergence of the individual. The freedom to move, to live, to express one's own self is one of the great outcomes of this revolution. And it is indeed a revolution, one that has infiltrated art, fashion, religion, business, and human relationships, and the consequences of it have affected our own considerations in the world of advertising. The debate about the youth market is academic. What is of concern

is a new generation of consumers who have experienced honesty and freedom in their development, who see hypocrisy and falsehoods, no matter how disguised. To reach them with advertising will require more than bright, shiny, tooth-filled smiles. The generation weaned on the vicarious experiences of movies could eagerly accept and embrace television and its promises. The "turned on" generation will require more. If we are to reach them, we must do it honestly and in a meaningful way.

The growth of discothèques, with their special environment of sound, light, color, slides, and films is an explosive, exciting force in our culture. Did it evolve from "happenings" of the art world or experiments in mixed media and film? In either case, it is an environment that completely stimulates the senses and, in so doing, creates an attitude of excitement and fun. Aspects of these environments have found their

way into the small, specialized boutique shops whose growth seemed to happen spontaneously. These shops generate an attitude, a life style, in the consumer. Retail stores had lost this feeling, and the boutiques have revived it. Department stores in turn have added boutiques. No longer is it sufficient to sell certain merchandise from counters, shelves, and racks in a nondescript atmosphere; the same merchandise becomes chic, modern, contemporary in a boutique environment. The consideration for the designer is how to apply this style of environmental retailing to other industries.

For example, should a supermarket have a special "food boutique," with unique fixtures, lighting, color, and the like? Should a gasoline station look like a racing pit or a space station, or become more feminine in color and appeal? Why are taverns changing their interiors to affect old English pubs? Must a diner look like a diner? What can be done to the roadside restaurant? The roadside motel? The roadside sign? The roadside?

Studies must be made to answer these questions. But designers should raise the questions at every opportunity. Existing concepts must not be taken for granted; they must be questioned, seemingly unrelated elements must be juxtaposed, and the results will spark new concepts and ideas.

One cannot but speculate what a chain of restaurants would look like if designed by Le Corbusier, Mies van de Rohe, Buckminster Fuller. How then would our landscape change?

The esthetics of the community need not be offended by selling; indeed they can be enriched.

One hundred million Americans have never flown, have never been inside an airplane, are not aware of the advantages and pleasures of flying. American Airlines has developed an exhibit, called the Astrosphere, to reach this audience where it is most accessible, at the shopping center.

Inside the Astrosphere a theater was designed to resemble the interior of an American Airlines 707 Astrojet. The seats, although set eight across as in airliners of the future, are duplicates of 707 seating. The visitors strap themselves into the seats, put on headsets, and watch a twelve-minute film about travel across America, including a pilot's eye view of both the landing and take-off. Stewardesses assist visitors, and travel literature is provided in seat pockets located in front of the passengers. This on-ground pre-conditioning of prospective passengers cannot help but stimulate their desire for air travel. Conservative American estimates forecast two million actual visitors to the Astrosphere and ten million people who will have seen it.

The Astrosphere is the largest dual-walled, air-inflated unit ever built. It has aproximately 6000 square feet of usable space, over half of which is used for visitor traffic flow and exhibit areas. Carried in four forty-foot vans, it can be set up in three hours.

The interior view shows the 128-seat theater in the center of the Astrosphere.

The cutaway model shows the plan of the Astrosphere. In the area outside the theater are exhibits by American Express Company, Hertz Rent-a-Car, Holiday Inns of America, and Texaco, all showing the relationship of these companies to travel. Domestic travel is promoted in keeping with the Discover America program established by President Johnson (see page 122). Flags surrounding the sphere are of the 50 states.

The American Airlines example of marketing at shopping centers to reach the consumer directly will inevitably be further developed by other companies. Shopping centers may soon become small world's fairs as marketers continue to cut the distance, be it physical or conceptual, between their product and the consumer.

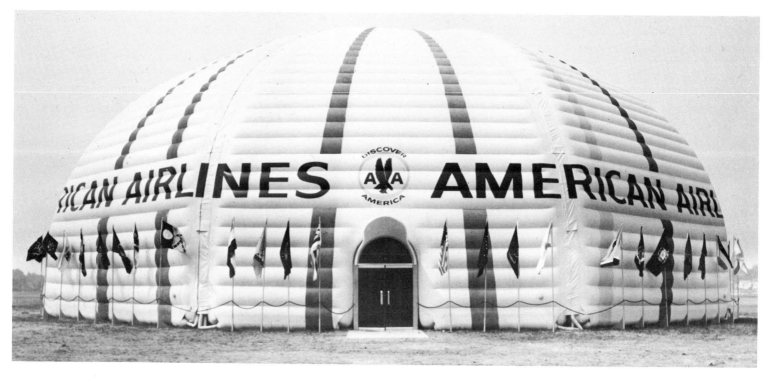

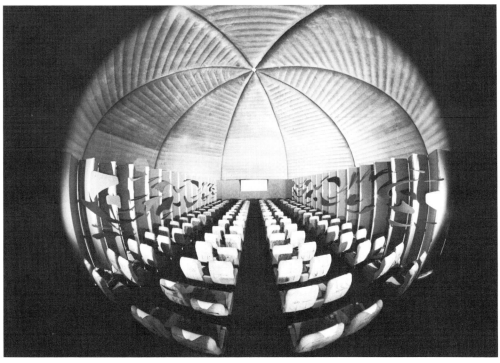

As we have seen in mobile exhibits, as well as the American Airlines Astrosphere, much effort is being made to reach the consumer directly with products or services. With the same motivation, Merrill Lynch, Pierce, Fenner & Smith has created an equally unique and highly successful exhibit in Grand Central Station. Called the Investment Information Center, it is equipped with the electronic displays designed by the Bunker-Ramo Corporation. The booth is staffed with account executives who answer questions and provide information to interested investors. In addition, they explain and demonstrate the services and facilities available through Merrill Lynch, hopefully converting prospects to customers. The electronic equipment in the exhibit can instantly retrieve information on 4400 stocks from the computers in Merrill Lynch's home office. The information appears in luminescent green characters on a wall-mounted electronic screen. The same data is printed on paper by a nearby Bunker-Ramo Teleprinter. Two adjacent screens show the live tickers of the New York and American Stock Exchanges in a display that reads like a page in a book instead of in the traditional horizontal tape format. Other electronic equipment provides information on business and financial news as well as over-the-counter issues.

The center occupies 400 square feet of space, of which approximately 175 square feet are taken up by equipment and furnishings, leaving 225 square feet of space for visitors. On the basis of a traffic study of people entering the exhibit on a typical day, Merrill Lynch projects well over one million visitors in a year. These represent a previously untapped reservoir of potential customers attracted with imagination and taste.

The choice of Grand Central for their facility is quite good. Thousands of commuters jam the station daily and represent affluent members of the community. While no stocks can be purchased at the exhibit, we may well consider this display a selling environment. Shown is a long view of the exhibit during an afternoon.

A close-up of the exhibit shows the judicious use of space, including clear glass doors, light-colored walls, unusually bright lighting, and clear, uncluttered design.

The Loft Candy Corporation sells packaged candies, toys, and gifts through company-owned stores in eastern markets but only through franchised dealers, primarily drugstores, in the midwest.

The expansion of the Loft chain into the midwestern market made desirable the development of a distinctive exterior appearance as well as an inviting interior. Moreover, the candy company desired to mass-merchandise their boxed candy for customer self-selection, a new concept in the area of bulk candy marketing. Quite obviously the interior had to be well planned, clean, and inviting in order to attract the consumer.

In keeping with the company's request, a pilot store was designed, staying within traditional lines of design, and built in Chicago. It was constructed with antique brick walls, natural cedar shake overhang, entrance carriage lights, and an awning in multi-width stripes of white, red, gold, and black.

The interior, with its simulated antique red brick floor, white columns, and early American tables and fixtures, reflects the mood of the outside. The total effect is warm and inviting. All the merchandise is clearly identifiable for easy self-service. The initial success of this pilot store was beyond expectations.

Total concern for visual marketing at the point of purchase is an all-inclusive responsibility. It requires involvement in exterior and interior design and signage as well as display fixtures and promotional merchandisers. To achieve an identity consistent with a corporate image requires planning and, above all else, management support for such an undertaking. It is indeed rewarding to have examples of such a continuing point-of-purchase program as is practiced by the Goodyear Tire and Rubber Company. The success of its total look is a constant reminder of the impact of the point-of-purchase medium under effective management. Indeed, it is the essence of all we are discussing in this book.

The scale-model suggested Goodyear dealership reflects sound understanding of the needs of the selling environment. Effectively transformed into reality are their actual counterpart in dealership in Memphis, Tennessee, and Stow, Ohio. Each unit, despite the varied locations, is unmistakably a Goodyear dealer, utilizing recommended Goodyear signage and outdoor merchandising techniques. The Memphis unit makes use of roadside visibility to display tires and service specials effectively. Both units use, in combination or separately, Goodyear designed and planned modular outdoor merchandisers to display tires. The Goodyear identification sign used in the Stow dealership is the latest redesign of the Goodyear logo.

The rectangular identification sign is another stage in the evolution of the Goodyear mark. More readable, flexible, and easier to fabricate, the new rectangular sign retains the Goodyear diamond and typography. Though modified, the sign retains the unique identifying marks that make the Goodyear logo well known and recognized by the public.

The service station is an increasingly important dealer in tires. The Goodyear model illustrates the suggested use of display material at the gasoline station.

Inside the dealership the center of interest in the salesroom is the complete tire department display, a custom unit developed to fit in the décor of shopping centers and mall-type shopping complexes as well as dealerships. Beneath each tire is an illuminated sign describing its qualities. The center panel (tire headquarters) is a two-sided motion unit that features current Goodyear advertising. The second photograph shows additional fixtures and displays usually used in dealerships in conjunction with the main tire display. Note that the end tire display matches the major tire display and functions in the same way.

The Goodyear national advertising merchandiser display is used as the center of attraction on the main tire wall. It can, of course, be used apart from the tire wall as an entity. The panels rotate, revealing a second advertising message. The panels are removable and new sets are provided throughout the year, so that the unit is continually current with national themes.

Two other tire display merchandisers are the premium tire stand, used with an illuminated feature display, and the two-sided display stand, featuring a large copy panel.

The interior considerations include floor color, signage, and the layout of selling areas. Shown here is the salesmen's closing area, which eliminates the need for extra closing rooms. The projector shows an interesting film about tires; thus, Goodyear utilizes the latest selling aids available.

The Goodyear Company considers every aspect of dealership needs, and supplies everything from information on how to store and stock tires to promotional displays, premiums, and similar point-of-purchase materials.

For example, a traditional event is the "Great Songs of Christmas" record sold through dealers. The complete in-store promotion includes a seven-foot floor display, a counter record merchandiser, window banners, and window posters.

No sale is complete without general merchandise bags and shopping bags, shown with their own display stand. Both are provided and decorated with the Goodyear logo. The source for all materials available as well as guidelines for point-of-purchase effectiveness is the Goodyear Merchandising System Guide. Throughout the book the dealer is encouraged to use the services of the Goodyear point-of-sale advertising department for guidance and assistance.

3 POINT-OF-PURCHASE DESIGN

DISPLAY DESIGN

To be effective in point-of-purchase, the designer must be knowledgeable in marketing and advertising. He is a member of a team, whose responsibilities are the marketing objectives of the company. He must know these objectives and the nature of the company's programs that are being developed to achieve them. He must be aware of the budgets being established and the advertising being planned. And he must be conscious of the values and selling points of those items he will be called upon to display. He then is responsible for the visualization of all of these goals.

The point-of-purchase designer, therefore, is not just designing a single piece for a single use in a single market. He is functioning in many areas and must know what is happening in all these areas to design effectively a point-of-purchase display.

This is not to say that the designer is a sales manager or a product manager or an advertising manager. But he must be aware of the information these people can provide to him so that he can create effectively. We see that the designer in point-of-purchase is not just an artist, whose sole concern is choice of color, typography, or art. Certainly he must employ these tools of his profession with effectiveness; but he cannot use them without the knowledge of how and where and why his display will be used.

The entire field of retailing is another area in which the designer should become knowledgeable. This is no small undertaking. Perhaps, in our background, some of us have worked in retail stores and are somewhat familiar with the demands of the store as well as the demands of the shopper. Naturally, we are all familiar with the problems of shopping in a supermarket or gasoline station or package store. We all function in these environments as consumers. But, as point-of-purchase designers, it now becomes our responsibility to understand retailing problems and to think not only in terms of aiding the retailer in his effort to sell merchandise, but of aiding, attracting, and selling to the consumer as well.

What are the problems of the retail drugstore, of the supermarket, of the gasoline station, of the package store? What are their display needs?

It is one thing to design a display in the confines of the drawing board. It is then another matter to decorate it and show it to the client, whether he be our own management (as in a company design department) or an outside producer. In either situation, the design is presented in an extremely unrealistic setting. What happens to this display when it functions in the retail store? Obviously, I cannot answer this question without surveying the entire retailing industry. I can only suggest that it would be wise for the designer to become familiar with the retail store in which his displays are used. Too often the experienced designer will forget how a field trip can serve him in his efforts to solve point-of-purchase problems effectively.

It would be beneficial for any company to expose and indoctrinate its design department by a tour of those retail outlets in which its merchandise is sold. It would be extremely beneficial for the designer to talk with the salesmen and the retailers in the field in different parts of the country, to get a feeling, a pulse, for those problems that he is being asked to solve.

It would be just as worthwhile for the designer to travel to his own company's manufacturing facilities to see the problems of manufacturing and of actual production. How does the merchandise have to be packed and shipped? What are the engineering problems, the assembly line difficulties, in getting merchandise into the display and getting the display packed and then shipped to the retailer?

There is a chain of events, a progression, and not one of these links can be forgotten. Each activity from the manufacture to the loading to the shipping to the unpacking to the display of the display must be considered. Each activity has its own problems that must be faced before any designer can consider his responsibilities at an end.

Many of these problems are marketing problems.

Yet they have everything to do with how effective your design will be. There are other people who are responsible for aspects of the problems we have posed. But they cannot solve them in the areas for which you, as the designer, are responsible. It is this particular aspect of your job that is your strength. It is important, therefore, that a company designer ask for information and be aware of all aspects related to his project. In this way, your responsibilities will not be relegated to deciding whether a display should be blue or green. You must be a contributing and integral member of the marketing group.

To many designers, these responsibilities may seem out of the realm of their interest and concern. But the point-of-purchase designer cannot disregard the objective of selling. We are perhaps the most commercial of the commercial designers. At the same time, we must not forget that we are designers who have to solve artistic problems. These problems must be solved effectively, creatively, and with excitement. That is the interest and challenge of our job: to portray graphically exciting photography, art work, and typography. Just like our colleagues in the agencies and studios we must solve these problems; but, unlike them, we function directly in the market place. And, therefore, we must utilize every conceivable weapon at our command. This, then, the market place, is our arena, and just how effectively we perform there will be reflected in our company's sales.

The creation of a display is a specific problem. There is no one way to begin, nor one approach correct for each industry. In many ways the methodology is similar for unlike industries and dissimilar for like industries. The needs of the individual advertiser become the most important criterion. Thus, we must reiterate the need for marketing information. Assuming we know our client, how then do we begin? What are the basic criteria for a display that a professional designer must know before his pencil touches paper? And, foremost, how does this information affect the form of the display?

The single most important consideration affecting design is budget. How much can be spent on the display? As we have seen, displays with similar merchandising features vary structurally because of the materials of which they are made (see merchandisers promotional and permanent). Thus, before we can think in terms of materials — wood, wire, plastic, or paperboard — we must know the amount of money allotted to a display.

Next, we must know the quantity of merchandise the display will hold, and, of course, we must have the merchandise in hand. We must know if the advertiser will pre-pack the merchandise or send the display to the store empty. Once we have the merchandise, we will determine the size and structure necessary to display and hold the product properly. Obviously, twelve glass containers pose a different problem than twelve cans. Yet the arrangement of twelve items is the beginning step in display design. Thus, (a) six wide, two deep; (b) four wide, three deep; (c) three wide, four deep are just three possibilities, each of which greatly affects the display design. For example, approach (a) gives you a wider area for a riser card, and thereby the opportunity for a bolder message, while approach (c) is narrower, and a possible solution where space is at a premium.

Once the layout of merchandise is determined, the structure develops. At about this stage the unit's design may be affected by the graphics of the package or other promotional considerations each of which must be taken into account.

The display concept arrived at is presented in sketch form; the sketches vary in finish from rough doodles to tight, comprehensive renderings. Once a display concept is decided upon, an actual-size model is made.

One last consideration, second only to budget in importance, is time. How many days, weeks, or months are allowed between the first sketch and the final manufactured display will affect the choice of materials used. Molding plastics is more time-consuming than die-cutting mountboard.

We see then that point-of-purchase designers cannot escape the realities of money, time, and technical expertise, each of which we may be wont to forget.

The Oasis display is an example of a unit that developed out of the uniqueness of its package. The hexagonal-shaped package inspired the design of the entire display, including its riser card. Seven packages stack and form their own hexagonal shape. The riser card reinforces the image, thereby creating a distinctive look.

The mechanics of the display are equally well conceived. The individual plastic triangular sections slide together to accept seven packages. Extruded aluminum parts lock the triangular sections, hold the riser card on top, and become legs for the display on the bottom. For greater display each unit locks into the others, and, used with a base, becomes a floor stand. This seemingly simple unit represents an extremely sophisticated design solution. The product, a foam flower holder, is graphically presented on an accompanying banner.

The introduction of Nine Flags Shaving Cologne represented a new concept in marketing men's colognes. Nine different essences, imported from different countries, were blended and bottled in the United States. Thus, the consumer was given an opportunity to experiment with different fragrances and vary their use at will. The colognes were packaged for sale as a complete collection, in combinations, or individually.

Design was an integral part of the development of the entire program. The tone of this prestigious line was set with the development of the package, and reflects the total involvement of designers from the initial marketing concept to the final in-store promotion. The line is an outstanding example of concern for the total look of all elements in the market place.

The package containing the entire collection is displayed in a stainless steel department store unit. The use of flags representing the nine countries adds color and interest to the display. Display testers were developed for use with individual fragrances or combination packages.

The principles that made Nine Flags a marketing success were employed in the development of My Islands Cologne for women. Once again, concern for the look at the point of purchase resulted in a handsome department store display. The brushed aluminum base holds the product (used for testing) on a revolving turntable. Displayed behind tinted blue-green plexiglas dividers are the package and its contents.

Many creative aspects of successful display design are often hidden. While, as graphic designers, our immediate attention is drawn to the graphic solution of a display, this is often a small part of the display's successful attributes. The true creativity of its solution may lie in its construction, its manufacture, its ability to be shipped, reused, or simply its display concept. The materials used to manufacture the display or its engineering may be the innovation that makes the display unique.

While graphics are an extremely important part of the display, it is the total effectiveness of a display that will measure its value in the marketplace—flexibility in terms of manufacture, use by the advertiser, and use at the retail level. A display that can occupy a small area yet hold much of the product, be attractive and an asset in the store is indeed an accomplishment.

Such is the case with the Calvert modular unit. This unit holds three dozen bottles of any Calvert brand, depending upon the reader attached to the display. The unit has more than one use, since it can store related snack items as well, thus increasing its value to the retailer. Moreover, the modular unit can be manufactured from one basic form in any quantity at any time. The cost of the molds for the injection-molded trays, initially defrayed, is no longer a factor on additional reorders of the unit. The design of the display is successful both as a merchandiser and in its ability to be manufactured.

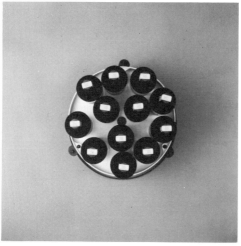

The design of a window display can be thought of as similar to stage design; in essence, one has to build a backdrop for the product. What is necessary is an idea that can be developed into a window. It may come from the package or from advertising, or it may represent a seasonal promotion. Once conceived, the idea is presented in sketch form. Often, as a complement to the sketch, a small miniature of the window is constructed; this is referred to as a mini.

Inherent in a professional designer's sketch is knowledge—knowledge about materials, production, manufacturing, and, as we have learned, merchandising. Therefore it is not surprising to see a rough sketch that is a realistic representation of the final display. Certainly there is much to be designed and redesigned during the display's development. However, the initial concept was clear and therefore became a workable reality. This is what we as point-of-purchase designers must strive for.

The following material illustrates some of the stages in the production of a Calvert Christmas window.

Shown are the sketch and the blank dummy construction. It is a large step from one to the other; the dummies are advanced constructions representing the final workable sample. Note the motor linkage and wiring necessary to achieve the side-to-side motion of the heads. The graphics are then applied directly to this dummy before presentation. The usual techniques of comprehensives are applicable, except in larger scale. Assuming a successful presentation, the next stage would be the preparation of finished art and mechanicals. The mechanicals are prepared flat and are drawn to specifications prepared by the finisher or printer. These specifications account for the position of parts of the art work in relation to size of printing presses and/or die-cutting equipment. The specifications will allow for bleed, tabs, and scores, and must be followed closely.

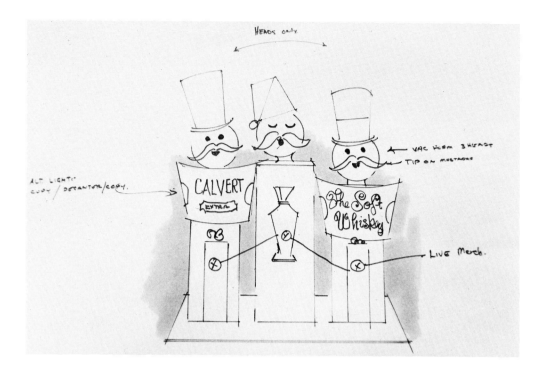

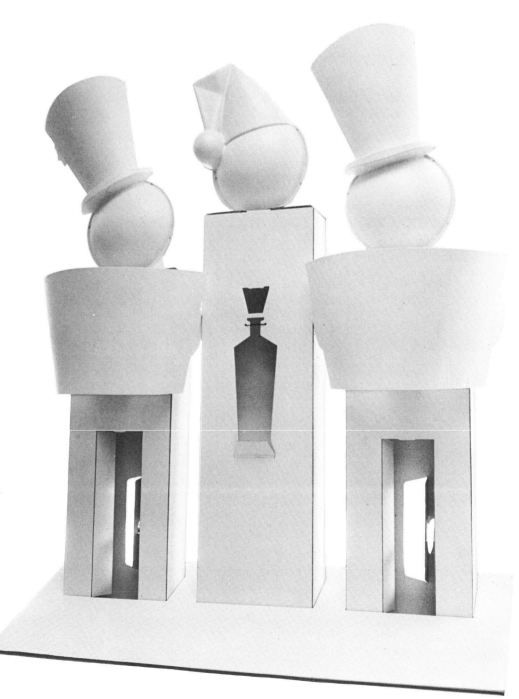

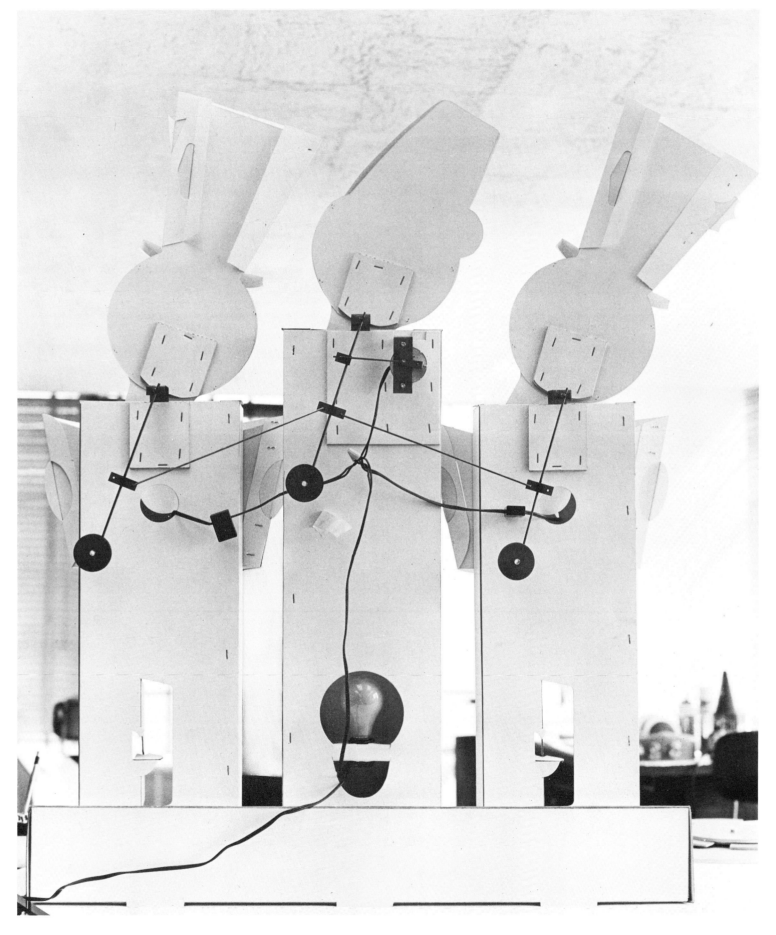

The complexity of the Calvert window and the nature of the various surfaces required many printing techniques. Therefore some surfaces were lithographed, while others were silk-screened.

Shown here are the flat pre-screened plastic sheets, the wooden mold onto which these sheets will be placed, and the vacuum machine, as well as the entire formed sheet. The formed heads will be die-cut in another machine. Of course, every area of the sheet is utilized.

Die making is one of the intricate operations of display finishing. Every tool is
custom-made for each job. The die
functions in several ways by cutting,
creasing, or scoring the display com-
ponents.

The steel rule, having been bent into
shape, is fitted onto a wooden surface.
Around the rule are resilient rubber
pads that push off the die-cut surface
from the die. The complex photograph
shown is a form for one of the figures
in the Calvert window.

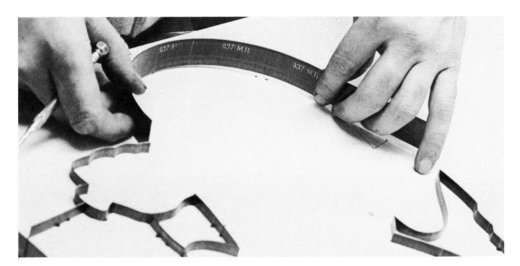

Display elements are assembled by glueing or stitching. Shown here are parts of the display being stitched.

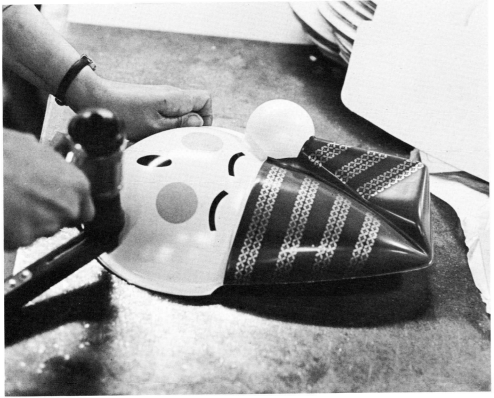

We have seen but a few of the many
steps in the production of a display.
Here is the final Calvert window. The
heads of the carolers move from side
to side, and, for further interest, the
opaline music sheets are illuminated.
The simple graphic treatment will stand
up well as a background for the richly
colored Christmas-wrapped merchandise used with the display.

Manufacturing

The display salesman is a vital link between the point-of-purchase manufacturer and the advertiser. He is the manufacturer's representative who sells the unique service of his organization to the advertiser. He is called in by the advertiser to solve specific point-of-purchase problems; the service is offered in return for a potential manufacturing order. The order to manufacture a unit is the result of a successful presentation made in competition with other point-of-purchase suppliers.

The designer who works for a point-of-purchase manufacturer usually gets his information from the salesman or sales manager within his own company. The sole source of his information is that which the salesman has derived from his client. The more effective the salesman is in eliciting information from the client, the greater is the knowledge available to the designer. Perhaps the future for designers in point-of-purchase is client contact, as part of a two-man sales team. This could be very helpful and save many false starts and wasted efforts.

As we have come to realize, you design differently for a pre-pack unit as opposed to a unit loaded by the dealer. A very simple question incorrectly answered completely wastes your time and energy. Perhaps your sketch can be adapted to work both ways, but the right way should be the way it was requested. The truly effective salesman will understand his position as communicator and display specialist and will therefore elicit the correct information. Creative selling is more than order taking and, in point-of-purchase, the knowledgeable salesman is a partner in design.

Display manufacturing is the keynote of the point-of-purchase industry. Inventiveness and creativity are a daily output of the producers. No display, no matter how simple, is without its own unique production problems. The ability to solve these problems in short periods is one of the strengths of the point-of-purchase industry.

Most often a display manufacturer will specialize in a particular aspect of point-of-purchase materials and supplement his needs outside of his own plant. That is, a manufacturer specializing in wire might buy the wood or plastic part of a display from another source. Many large shops can handle all aspects of manufacturing, including wood, wire, and plastic. Others specialize in finishing and die-cutting, others in corrugated board, metal, and so forth. There are trade shops that work directly for brokers or other display manufacturers. The point-of-purchase industry, like all industries, has giant producers along with small operations. What they all must have in common in order to survive, regardless of their size, is the ability to produce quality work on schedule.

The planning of display manufacturing is an amazing feat. A display constructed of wood, wire, and metal must be planned from the first cut of wood to the total assembly of all elements. All the parts must merge to become one display unit. The assembly of the display is usually done by hand, and therefore involves human engineering problems as well as technical ones. All these factors must be accurately estimated so that a display production schedule can be maintained.

Unlike other manufacturers, display producers tool up for production that terminates within weeks, yet their plans are as thorough as if they were producing on a yearly basis. They are responsible for unique technical innovations as well as fundamental marketing ideas at the point of purchase.

The designer quite obviously cannot function without a basic knowledge of display materials and their manufacture. Perhaps you have cut and scored paperboard, nailed and glued wood, and even worked with wire and welding. Equipped also with a basic understanding of plastic manufacturing, the designer can begin to have a feel for materials. At the very first opportunity, the designer should visit various manufacturing facilities to see first-hand the

development of a display. The experience is invaluable and will immediately answer many questions about display design. Certainly, the agenda should include mounting and finishing plants, wood, wire and plastic manufacturers. Obviously, in areas of special concern the field trip is a must as well. For instance, the creation of a sign requires the close cooperation of the designer, engineer, and manufacturer, and much can be learned from a study of the manufacturer's facilities. It seems basic, but it cannot be overemphasized: the field trip is invaluable. It is as rewarding as your first visit to a typographer or printer. Inspiration is not found only at the drawing board.

Throughout the book we have made reference to plastic displays. These displays are generally vacuum-formed or injection-molded. It would be appropriate at this point to discuss briefly these processes. They are indeed an important ingredient in point-of-purchase structures, and will be even more so in the future.

A plastic is any of a group of synthetic or natural organic materials which, when soft, can be permanently formed, generally under pressure accelerated by the application of heat. The newly created form retains its shape when cooled. Just what plastic to use depends upon the nature of the job, whether the display will be used outdoors or indoors, the kind of illumination, and the method of manufacturing. Plastics vary by chemical formulation as well as by brand names. (Two acrylic plastics most commonly known are Lucite and Plexiglass, manufactured respectively by E. I. du Pont de Nemours and Co. and Rohm and Haas Co., Inc.)

The properties of all plastics are the concern of experts. Obviously it would be far afield for the designer to specify the type and brand of plastic unless he has extensive background in this field. He should know the effect he wants and use that as a guide in the development of the display.

Vacuum-forming is the fastest and most economical method for producing a three-dimensional item. In this method a sheet of plastic is clamped in a frame, heated, and drawn down by a vacuum into a mold. Vinyls and cellulosics are materials most readily adaptable to vacuum-forming. Vinyls are most versatile in fabrication as well as decoration. The original sheet of plastic can be metalized, printed, sprayed, or hot-stamped before forming. Thus the copy and decoration are applied directly to the plastic as needed.

Injection-molding is a more costly and time-consuming method of forming plastics. In this fabrication, pellets or granules are fed from a hopper into a long-heating chamber called an injection cylinder. The softened material is forced by an injection ram, at high pressure, through a nozzle, from which it is injected into a cold mold. Upon cooling, the mold is opened and the finished form is released.

The designer should bear in mind that plastics have their own inherent qualities and look. This is an asset if the designer emphasizes these characteristics. Too often plastics are used to imitate other materials. While they can simulate glass or wood, they are not restricted to the same forms that these materials have to take because of their composition. As in all our other endeavors, creativity is the added ingredient.

In studying point-of-purchase display, it is valuable to devote equal attention to the utilization of materials as to design and graphics. The Helena Rubinstein display is a good example of combining many materials to create a display. Though a promotional unit of short life, much effort went into its design, so that it could successfully merchandise various products.

Starting at the top, the riser card is printed in six-color lithography. The V-shaped center panel is foil mounted to paperboard. The carton and tall lipstick are attached to the center panel with a clear plastic holder. The base is vacuum-formed plastic, molded to hold both lipsticks and glass containers. The price strips attached to the base and the background on the wings were printed with the reader. The shade charts were printed separately in letterpress, then mounted to the display. The result of all the various materials and processes was a singularly handsome display, all elements of which contributed to the total effect.

The quality-control efforts of a designer do not necessarily end with the release of a job to production. Any material in a display should come under his scrutiny for final approval. The vacuum-form tray, the hot-stamping—whatever the detail, it is the designer's responsibility to see that the manufacturing of the display piece follows his specifications exactly.

Once the job is properly reproduced, the next step is mounting it. Again, a hand-made sample is presented to you. Then the printed sheet is mounted and

die-cut for your approval. This, too, is checked against the mechanical to see that the edges, shapes, and forms created are properly die-cut, with scores in the right place. After all corrections are made, the sample is returned to the finisher, who will then proceed with correcting his dies. In large quantity runs, the very first samples that are finished, mounted, scored, and die-cut should again be sent to you for approval, just to double-check that something is not inadvertently overlooked. It is always easier to make a change before a job is completed than after.

When we speak of the production of a display, we must not overlook the importance of the production personnel in the purchasing and manufacturing of the unit. It is their responsibility to be able to provide the correct material and construction in which a given display will take form. From a production point of view, if you are working with a man who is inspired and cares, who is an innovator and feels a sense of identification with the final result, you will have a valuable partner.

Quite often, a designer has created something that is impractical, yet, with a little more effort on the part of the purchasing or production department, a seemingly impractical problem can indeed be solved. Designers must always think in terms of what can be and should be done. A close working relationship between production and design is essential, in order to take advantage of technological advances in the industry.

HOLIDAY EYES

EVERYDAY'S A HOLIDAY WITH

Helena Rubinstein's

HOLIDAY MAKE-UP

HOLIDAY LIPS

LONG-LASH

The First Mascara and Lash-Builder in one! Actually adds length... adds thickness as it colors! 2 50 REFILL 1 50

4 EYE-FLATTERING SHADES.
With Long-Lash Mascara—you won't believe your eyes!

Black	Dark Brown
Brown	Navy Blue

8 NATURAL-LOOKING COMPLEXION SHADES.
Won't streak. Won't discolor.

Peach Ivory	Crackerjack
Ivory Rachel	Soft Beige
Blushing	Golden Beige
Rose Peach	Bronze

FASHION STICK

The fabulous, long, slim lipstick and lipliner in one! Gives a perfect outline as it colors! 1 50 REFILL 1 10

24 HOLIDAY SHADES.
Creamy, enriched formula keeps your lips dewy soft.

PASTEL

BRIGHT

DEEP

Silk Fashion LIQUID MAKE-UP SOFT BEIGE — Helena Rubinstein

Silk Fashion LIQUID MAKE-UP GOLDEN BEIGE — Helena Rubinstein

Silk Fashion LIQUID MAKE-UP CRACKERJACK — Helena Rubinstein

SILK FASHION Liquid Make-Up. The exclusive dimensional make-up that brings your prettiest features into focus! 1 75

New WEDDING RING LIPSTICK in Classic Golden Cases.

Motion

The opportunity to design with motion is a special challenge—a challenge that represents one more of the manifold ways in which a designer functions in point-of-purchase. How well he functions depends on his technical knowledge of the mechanics of motion, and, more important, his ability to think of motion in its own inherent terms.

Research consistently shows that motion attracts attention and is responsible for increasing the sale of the merchandise displayed. That this is true is not a surprise. Life, today, abounds in motion; it is where no motion exists that an unreal situation is created. Naturally, something that moves stands apart from something that does not. The concern of the designer is to utilize this advantage and to maintain it when competition increases.

The windmill, weather vane, pin wheel, and mobile are synonymous with motion—free motion, as it were, which relies on nature for its source of power. Natural motion has been used in point-of-purchase as well. But our needs are too demanding; our motion must be predictable, reliable, and controllable.

Technically, the development of battery motors has paralleled the development and needs of the point-of-purchase industry. As the need for more sophisticated motors became apparent, it was answered by the motion industry. Each thereby contributed to the growth of the other. Thus, we have seen development from a very simple oscillating motor, whose function is to move a few ounces of paperboard back and forth,

to "start and stop" motion motors, to rotary motors. With electric current motors, these multi-action motions can be readily achieved. But in battery-operated units, often no bigger than your hand, this is an achievement—an achievement that continues to put new, inexpensive motors at the disposal of the designer.

Technological advances have enabled the designer to think in terms of active light as well as motion. Transistorized flashers have a time sequence which can be modified to fit the needs of the display and its motion. Sound, too, is at his command. Olfactory experiments may soon unleash still another area of expression. Technological developments are rapid, and the designer must be alert to them if he is to function imaginatively.

What is the proper utilization of motion? Too often we have seen a moving hand pointing to a product, the moving product display, moving concentric circles. All these are presumably classified as motion units, but they do not represent effective motion design. A still piece that moves is not motion design; a display properly designed for motion does not function if it is *not* in motion. A Calder mobile in a vacuum is perhaps a good piece of sculpture. But a Calder working with subtleties of wind, time, and motion is something else again. A design thought of in terms of motion will be a more effective design than a still piece that is made to move.

Some of the **sources** of unique thinking about motion as well as light can be

found in the works of the kinetic sculptors. Their utilization of electric motors, light, sound, and electronics are inspiring, esthetically, as well as for technological innovations. The playback between the arts and technology often produces simultaneous results in fine art and applied art. Thus, polarized screens have been effectively utilized both in art galleries and in back-bar tavern displays. The problem in both arenas is to use it creatively.

The practical considerations in creating a motion display are many. Foremost, can your concept work? Is it practical as well as economical? The motor manufacturer's sales representative is your partner in this venture. He should be called in at the start, so that he can advise and guide the development of the working motion display. Sufficient time must be allowed for the development of non-standard motors. The manufacturing schedule of the display and the manufacturing schedule of the motor must be properly coordinated. The display dummy and the final approved construction on which final motor tolerances are made must be made available to the motor producer to work with.

Once again we are illustrating a point-of-purchase project that requires the effort of the designer and his production man, as well as sales representatives of the display and motor manufacturers. At the least, we have a team of four men trained to solve display problems. The designer working effectively with this group can see his concepts realized.

The Milshire pole topper is two-sided. A specially developed motion device turns the panels 180 degrees, pauses briefly while the message is read, and then quickly turns them back to reveal the other illustration. The display shows a strong product visual as well as a party scene.

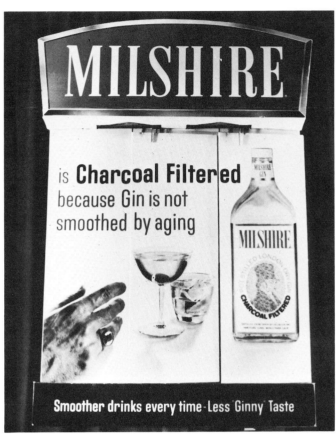

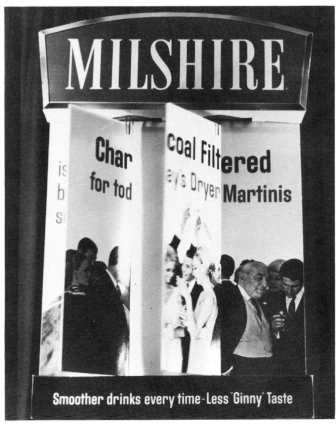

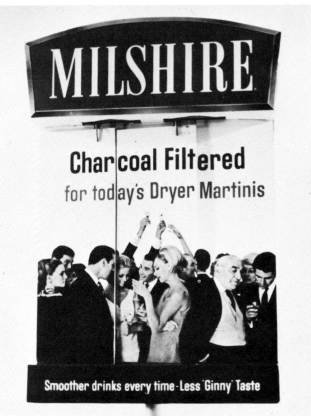

The battery-operated motor is the work horse of motion in point-of-purchase. Shown here are three motors whose motion action can accommodate most display requirements. Bear in mind that each display requires its own linkage, or connection from the motor to the moving parts of the display. The linkage problem is solved in conjunction with the motor manufacturer.

Motor (A) uses a simple rocking motion. It can run continuously for weeks on its single flashlight battery. The unit is engineered to use gravity and like-pole repulsion to produce the non-stop motion. Thus, power is used a small part of the actual time, extending the battery life.

Motor (B) is adaptable to many different swinging motions. It can do a full swing or be adapted to various degrees of speed and action.

Motor (C) is a rotary motor that operates at any angle, including upside down. Additionally, it can be wired for clockwise or counterclockwise rotation, with variable speeds of one to one hundred fifty r.p.m.

A

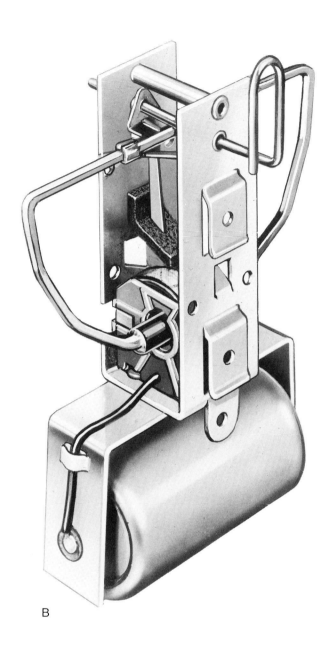

B

C

The Diamond Walnut gingerbread cookie is a delightful pole topper. The head swings from side to side while the arms and legs move up and down.

The Carling Black Label display is a ferris wheel; the six-pack case was well adapted to this structure.

The nuttiest cookies wear DIAMONDS!

DIAMOND WALNUTS

Here are two electrically motorized Polaroid displays. The egg-shaped display is molded plastic. The camera revolves, demonstrating the manner in which the finished picture is removed from it. The front of the unit has its own spotlight focusing on the camera area.

The pentagon-shaped display is an equally well conceived unit. The three sections are molded plastic. Designed to be the same size and shape, they are made from one mold. Each section is lighted from inside by three bulbs; the lights in the top section spotlight the cameras as well. The top section revolves to the left, the middle section to the right, and the bottom remains stationary. The effect is a well-lighted, modern, revolving showcase.

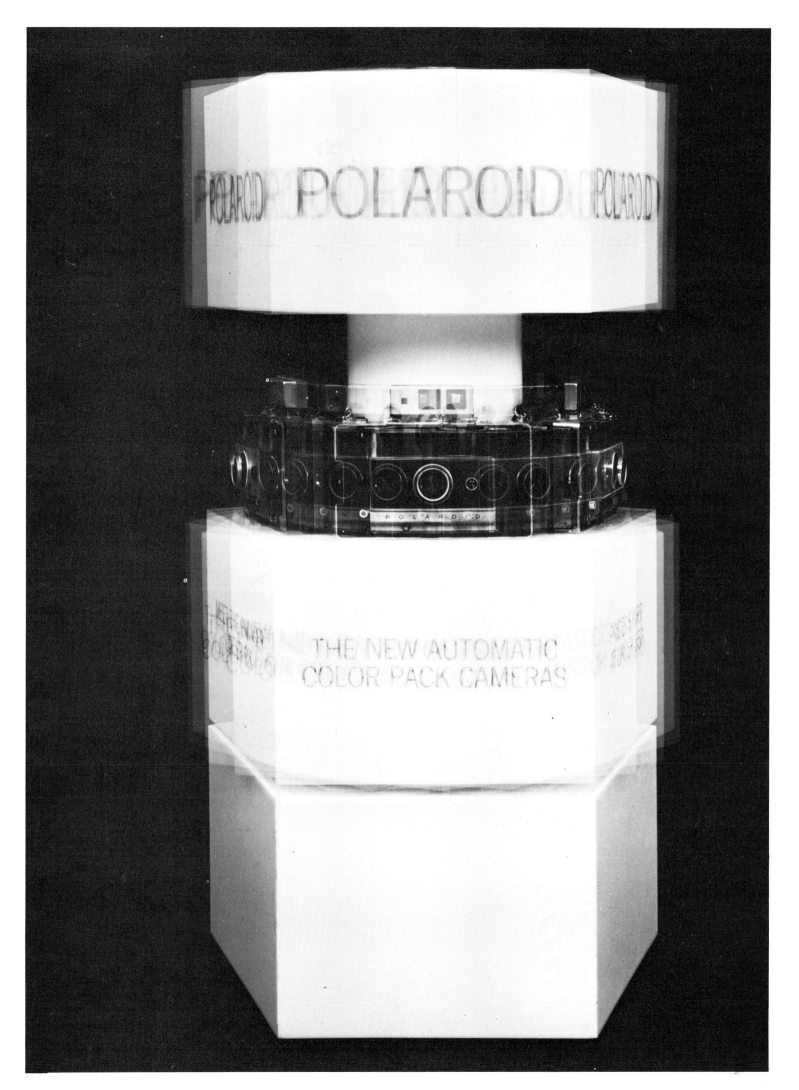

The use of audio devices in point-of-purchase is somewhat in its early stages. With increased demands for audio, it will only be a short time before it is as commonplace as motion.

One successful unit features a commercial by actor Arthur Treacher. Consumer-activated, the audio device, measuring $3\frac{1}{2}''$ by $3\frac{1}{2}''$ by $4\frac{5}{8}''$, weighing eight ounces, and powered by a single D-cell battery, plays for twenty-six seconds. The unit, used with stacking cases, is functional, and it ties in well with national advertising.

There are many elaborate and costly audio-visual units on the market, many of which are utilized in point-of-purchase. These are not as yet used on a mass level, but this is certain to happen. Perhaps tomorrow's display will use film strips and sound tracks supplied to a store's existing point-of-purchase audio projector.

The potential of this equipment in point-of-purchase is an exciting challenge for the designer. He may well find himself creating story boards like his counterpart in television. Or perhaps he will be involved in mixed media at the store level.

Counterparts of this back-bar display are found in galleries and museums. The ethereal changing color forms are the center of interest. Ever commercial in its use, the display has a message placed directly in the middle of the color happening. A half-rounded, molded-plastic replica of the J & B bottle is mounted to the display; a light inside the bottle serves to highlight it. The use of light and motion is extremely effective in the back-bar environment for which this display was designed.

GRAPHIC DESIGN

Design as a personal statement of the designer is wrong.

Design as a style is wrong.

Design for design's sake is wrong.

Type for typography's sake is wrong.

Photography as art is wrong.

Illustration as art is wrong.

What then is right? Design that communicates its message in a technique suitable for that message.

My point is really simple. We have a responsibility to communicate a message. Within the framework of design, there are endless ways in which a design solution can be satisfied. But, before an approach is decided upon, it should be questioned in terms of its rightness as a solution for the particular problem. A strong photograph, illustration, bold copy—each must relate to the specific problem. And, most of all, the final solution must be in a format or design style that is in keeping with the character of the job.

The clean Swiss look is not the answer to every problem, no matter how much it has been embraced by designers. This look is smart and extremely contemporary, but is not universally applicable as a layout solution. In its indiscriminate use as a style are the seeds of decreasing effectiveness and, therefore, eventual demise. It may well be the hallmark of the sixties, but it should never be the ultimate design style. There is no final solution in design. Searching for new expressions in communications is what good graphic design is all about.

What kind of graphic design is applicable in the marketplace? Hopefully, good design which tastefully and effectively communicates its message.

We have discussed all the variables that affect the decision as to the style of design. But what must always be present is the touch of design. Our survey of various industries suggests a varying pattern of taste. This is a good barometer of the individual company's concern for design. Those companies which seek good design get it. The others require greater communication between the designer and marketing so that good graphic design at the point of purchase can be achieved. The impetus for such action must come from the designer and the design industry. There is sufficient evidence of the value of design in the market place to justify the designer's efforts. Unfortunately, the case must still be presented to those in management who have not quite understood that good design is necessary in all industries.

Effective graphic design in point-of-purchase depends on many factors, factors that may parallel other mediums of advertising but are unique to this industry. Environment is the foremost concern of the designer. Where will the display be used?

In no other area of graphic design is environment as important as in point-of-purchase. An advertisement can be a double-page spread, thereby completely dominating a visual area. A direct-mail piece, when held in the hand, is fulfilling its function, and stands on its own merits. The package, of course, is designed with consideration for its place on the shelf against competition. But it, too, when removed from the shelf, stands on its own merits in the hands of the consumer.

Only the point-of-purchase display remains constantly within the atmosphere it was designed for. Only the point-of-purchase display stands consistently surrounded by its own competition. The display's success is the ability to stand out and sell its product.

Where will the point-of-purchase display be used? How will it be used? How will it be seen—hurriedly passed in a supermarket, or deliberately studied in a department store boutique, or subliminally noted in a tavern? Will it be seen on the move as you ride past a service station, or viewed as the car is serviced? Each store has its own unique selling psychology. And, within each store, the consumer is in a different frame of mind. These considerations must affect our graphic decisions.

With what advertising theme is the product associated? Can it be used effectively at the point of purchase? What is the nature of the product? Can we build around it or just complement it? Perhaps the product sells itself (the aspiration of every advertiser), and all we need is a complementary display sign. However the problem presents itself, the graphic solution becomes a design problem. As a design problem, it is related to all other layout methods, devices, and concepts.

I have assumed that my reader is a professional designer or is at least familiar with the means of graphic expression. Thus, these pages discuss the tools of graphic design only as they differ in relation to point-of-purchase.

One of the tools of great import in point-of-purchase graphics is color. Strangely enough, it is the simplest problem to relate and the most complex to solve.

Great or even good colorists are few in number. Even among contemporary artists of the past hundred years—at a time when color exists on its own as the subject of a painting—many are good colorists, few are great. Some of the great names of modern art limit their palettes to the primary colors (thus eliminating personal choice), and many schools of design have emerged in this tradition. To use color in painting is an extremely personal expression, rooted within the artist, based on his own taste and intuition. The color diagrams and rationalizations of the art historians come after the fact.

How then do we use color in the market place? Perhaps with intuition, primarily with information. Fundamental information about color is a part of every designer's education. We know that warm colors advance, cold colors recede. We know what percentage of the people like blue and what percentage prefer red. We know that our culture affects our color preferences. Blue for boys, pink for girls. Brides in white, mourners in black. We know that efficiency in offices and factories has been improved by the use of color. Experimentation and research about color continually expand our knowledge, and yet good colorists are few.

One of the most important considerations about color in point-of-purchase is the environment in which it will be used: outdoors, day or night; indoors, with fluorescent or incandescent light; in a tavern or supermarket, or a drugstore. A single color researched as the "people's favorite" cannot function equally well in all those environments. And should there be such a color, chances are that someone else is already using it, limiting the distinctiveness of your solution. (How many more red, white,

and blue signs can there be?) This is why I have largely refrained throughout this book from specific color references in describing materials shown. It would be of little use to know that yellow and blue or ochre and cerise made a given display successful, without knowing everything else about the display's use.

With color, the designer must be a juggler, balancing personal taste, current vogue, cultural preferences, environment, and usage in order to find the right answer. None of these items is in themselves unchanging. Today, men's fashions include colors that were the woman's domain less than a decade ago. Automobile colors follow the rainbow. Airplanes are multicolored. Again, as in every other aspect of point-of-purchase design, the designer must be aware of all that occurs around him. We know that color in the market place is a vital selling aid when used effectively. Be free to explore the potential of the selling power of color. But handle with care.

While we are considering color as it applies to the individual unit, there is another area of concern that should be considered: its use in the market place. Color is a powerful stimulus when used environmentally. Its application at the point of sale is a challenge.

Color alone can guide a consumer's progression through space. For example, a supermarket can color-code its interior to aid the progression of the consumer through the store; this might include the shelf, end aisle, ceiling, or floor. Color-coding of selling areas is equally applicable to drugstores and other multidepartmented stores.

Recently, an airline painted its planes for identification as well as for decoration. Coupled with brilliant advertising, a new use of color was initiated. This same principle can be applied endlessly to any activity. The use of accepted colors need only be questioned, and innovations become realities.

The Polaroid Swinger carton is an excellent example of using color in relationship to the market place as well as for its own decorative value. Elsewhere in the book we have noted that three facings of the square carton are in blue, green, and cerise respectively, and three are in black. Stacked in any combination, the colors work well with one another and create a colorful display, a display of packaging that can stand apart in store windows and store interiors dominated by Kodak yellow. The fact of Kodak yellow in the market place became the first consideration of the designer when working on his own color selections.

Typography is as varied in its application in point-of-purchase design as in any design area. All the rules and nuances of good typographic design are applicable. The type solution should depend more on the right style for the display and its packaging than on the dictates of current typographic style. What will be important is not so much which of the type faces is decided upon as how effectively and tastefully it will be used. The paramount consideration is legibility. A display is read quickly and every effort must be made to aid in the comprehension of the message. Color in type should enhance the attractiveness of the display, but not at the expense of legibility (that is, unless we are involved in psychedelic materials).

Since type in point-of-purchase is used in display sizes, some technical demands should be considered. For example, in enlarging type for reproduction, letter spacing may become too open. An aid to the problems of size in point-of-purchase use is film lettering. Film type is excellent for its sharp clear type, which can be blown up 300 or 400% without blurred edges. The designer should be aware of what happens to type as he works with it in large sizes. If the finished mechanical is not made to true reproduction size, a photostat should be made to see what the type looks like when blown up.

The designer must also be aware of the process by which his message will be printed. With lithography, he can count on fidelity to his mechanical art work. In preparing art for printing with rubber plates on corrugated board, one might expect some fuzziness developing around the edges of the type, particularly in reverse panels. The quality can be controlled, but the equipment is not yet so perfect that fuzziness will not occur. Therefore, any serif type under 18 point might be replaced with a gothic type with at least the weight of a News Gothic. This is not a rule, but a precaution. It is applicable to silk-screen printing as well. When copy is prepared to be hot-stamped, you can expect a small amount of shrinkage. Again, in embossing on plastic, there is a tendency for the letters to become filled out and look heavier than they are. In both cases, gothic faces suffer the least by distortion.

Logos designed specifically for use on packages do not automatically work on a display. They may be too fine to read. When enlarged, though, they may lose their charm and proportion. They may be weak; they may just not feel right. If the logo is necessary—and certainly the marketing identification is increased with it—then the logo must be modified for display use.

Thus, if the designer is aware of the mechanics of reproduction and works within its framework and limitations, he can create notable typography at the point of sale.

This counter card makes good use of white to offset the heavy illustration. The Lucrezia Borgia record album cover projects three-dimensionally in front of its background. Of equal contrast to the ornate typography on the record album is the film-lettered Futura. Clean, crisp, and currently in vogue, it represents a thoughtful approach to a typographical problem at the point of purchase.

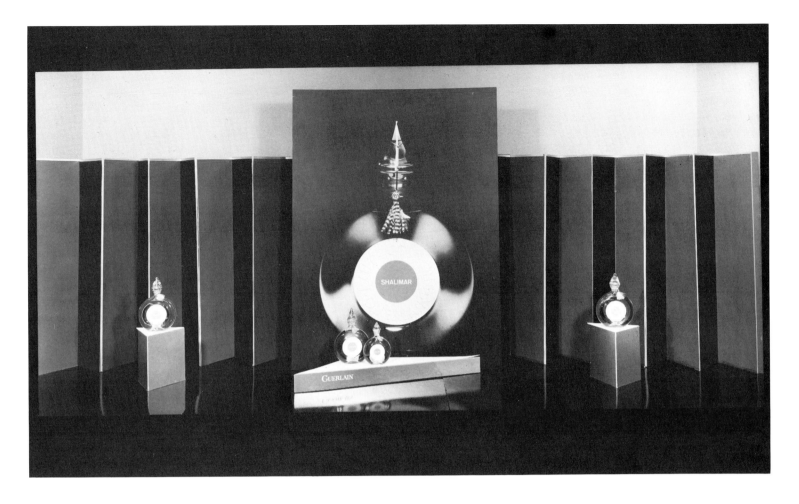

Photography is a strong element in today's advertising. "One picture is worth 10,000 words" is more than an artist's vindication. In store selling, it is a reality of our everyday experience. If we can project the same photograph from the magazines and television to the retail store, the opportunity for recognition is tremendously improved. If we must begin apart from national advertising, the photographic solution becomes a new problem. Here, too, we design around the kind of photographic image that will best do the selling job. Hard or soft sell, rational or romantic—whatever the reason, it must be the right choice for the job.

What is the appropriate image depends upon the same factors we have been discussing. In photography and illustration, the designer sets the tone of the message by his choice of photograph, cropping, layout, and the like; these factors are the same for point-of-purchase as for other advertising media.

Technically, we generally are working on a large scale; therefore, the photograph will require more retouching and attention to details. Moreover, we have better control of reproduction, due to our specifications of printing techniques. In many ways the photograph in point-of-purchase can be carried further than in other media, enhancing its qualities. This is true of illustration and its use at the point of sale as well.

The Shalimar photograph is outstanding—an extremely beautiful full-color still life that suggests the romance of the perfume. It was used effectively in national advertising and translated equally well to the point of purchase, in this case a window display. Very little had to be done to embellish this visual.

The Kate Smith portrait is a warm and loving illustration of this great lady. This twenty-by-thirty-inch counter card effectively employs illustration in an industry prone to photographic portraits of its stars.

To speak of design as a graphic tool seems a paradox. Yet, I mean it here as an expression that represents the solution to a graphic problem. By using a symbol or design, a solution is arrived at that is in itself the answer to the problem. Design as its own visual requires excellent taste and control to be used effectively in competition with photography and illustration. The Chicago Great Lake poster is such an example. A cool blue background is the only color used in this handsome poster.

chicago has a great lake

We have explored graphic design as it relates to point-of-purchase. The examples presented in this book have been used to illustrate a specific area of the point-of-purchase medium. In so doing they have been isolated from their own supporting promotional materials. In most instances, displays are part of a complete promotional program. Materials prepared in support of a promotion may include dealer selling sheets and other selling aids used to explain the promotion to the dealer. In support of the program are in-store selling aids and perhaps consumer give-aways. All are a part of a program; quite obviously, they should all relate to each other. The Polaroid Swinger materials, which include a window display, counter cards, streamers, and two-sided overhangs, are an example of this kind of promotion.

Printing

The designer familiar with printing problems in advertising will find himself with similar problems in point-of-sale. The preparation of art for printing remains basically the same. Letterpress, offset, lithography, silk-screen, photogelatin, and xerography are printing methods that are used in point-of-purchase. The quantity of the run, the subject being reproduced, the costs, and the use, all determine the printing method to be employed. Perhaps the art work dictates flat, bold colors, which are best reproduced in silk-screen, or halftones, best reproduced in offset and letterpress. As we have stated, the designer must be aware of the potential of his medium through every point-of-purchase activity. The basics of the decision are not overly complex. More often than not, the designer will be working primarily in one medium. It is within the framework of the selected printing method that the designer can exercise control and achieve unusual results.

The responsibilities of a conscientious designer do not end when the art work is released to the production department. In order fully to guarantee an effective job, it is his responsibility to supervise many of the steps before the final completion of the display. While much of the detail and follow-through work will be handled by the production or purchasing department, there are many decisions that must be made by the designer.

A simple thing like checking a blueprint of a job, which to the non-designer may seem adequately prepared, may show incorrect positioning of type, incorrect size of art work, or broken type. The designer, therefore, should be very conscientious in his effort to check blueprints or proofs when they are submitted for approval. Lest he forget some aspect of the job, he should check every blueprint or proof against his mechanical. In the final analysis, this will show him exactly what he wants.

Depending upon the nature of a given job, the designer should be available to check the design while it runs on the press. This is not to say that every job that runs requires a designer's presence or must be supervised by the designer himself. However, he or a member of his department should be present when a job of critical nature runs, so that any variation in color and tone can be interpreted from the designer's point of view, in relation to the reproduction he desires. It is not a decision to be left to a pressman or to your production man. It is your decision, and your responsibility, to see that the best reproduction is achieved.

In display work, where shipping and handling are important factors, most printing surfaces are varnished to prevent scuffing. Once again, this is a decision that can affect the final appearance of the job. Varnishes vary in effect from mat to high-gloss, including lamination. The use of each varies with the job. The concern about varnish is its effect on the halftone and colors to which it is applied. While varnish may be useful, the unvarnished sheet should come as close to the original art work as possible. Just as in a painting, a varnish aids and unifies the surface. It also can yellow, but the yellowing of a varnish can be controlled by its formulation. The designer must make his needs known to the printer.

In all printing there is the potential for creating something new, for getting a different look. It can be accomplished in many ways. Perhaps the job can be run on special stock, such as foil, or with special inks, such as fluorescents. Possibly the screen can be increased in size beyond its normal usage. Possibly the blue plate can run in yellow and the black in blue. What are the results?

It is easy to run two-color jobs and then get a third or fourth by mixing bendays and overprinting—this is fundamental and basic. It is beyond this simple tech-nique that the designer can effect a different look, by questioning the conventional procedures.

There are many photo-mechanical techniques of converting tone copy to line. For the experimental designer and lithographer this can be achieved with the lithographer's facilities. By shooting tone copy as if it were live art, a high-contrast line print can be created. This technique can be helpful in converting a weak photograph into a strong graphic image.

Here is an example of a weathered barn reproduced in halftone and line.

4 SOURCES AND RESOURCES

The course of this book has been practical and filled with the concerns of the commercial world of the designer. I have assumed that the quest for visual stimulation would be an ingredient for which the reader would be responsible. It would be his inner need to search for and discover his own oasis of creativity and inspiration. Certainly, to innovate we must find our inspiration outside of our own arena of concern, or we repeat or modify that which has already been done. So it is expected that today's designer will be found in museums and galleries, seeking out that which refreshes the spirit.

How deeply involved the designer will be in this world of art in no small way reflects on his success in the commercial world. At times it is hard to separate the two. The point remains that all that is around us can at some time be expressed in our work. It is this interplay that is the excitement of point-of-purchase design.

Following is a potpourri of design garnered from different sources that fall within this framework.

The Aluminum Company of America commissioned this structure as part of a program of designs for the future in aluminum. The solar toy is a brilliant, colorful plaything that spins, wheels, and cranks to create a delightful display of motion and sound powered only by the sun's rays. Designed by Charles Eames, it draws electric energy from selenium cells in an aluminum-sheet reflector. The solar toy is an imaginative adventure by an imaginative designer and company.

People Chairs is a collection of fun furniture designed by Jay Doblin for the Aluminum Company of America. Created to explore the use of aluminum and possible finishes in the design of outdoor furniture, they are not commercially available. The designer chose to find the solution to a chair body out of one piece of aluminum, with no waste, minimum bends and folds, and a material that is indestructible in the face of weather. His objectives were well satisfied.

Recently, designer Shiego Fukuda exhibited a show called Toys and Things at the IBM Gallery in New York. It was a joyful exhibition filled with delightful surprises: toys as playthings or objects of joy, things of use or not. They are just pleasurable three-dimensional expressions, some of which are illustrated.

In each instance the craftsmanship is exemplary. Every form is a thoughtful individual expression that works with the whole form. The negative is as meaningful as the positive, particularly the tree of life with its own birds. The ping-pong balls were decorated with fabric tails and exhibited in a fish tank. Floating, they made random patterns of color and texture. The designer's flat graphic books somehow convey a feeling of three dimensions, and many pages in fact fold out into surprising shapes. The entire show was a maximum of expression with a minimum of means.

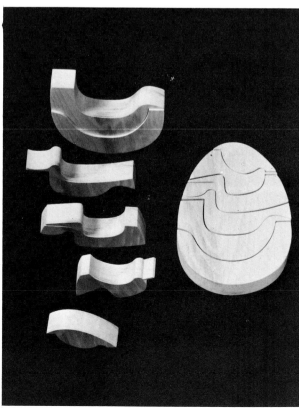

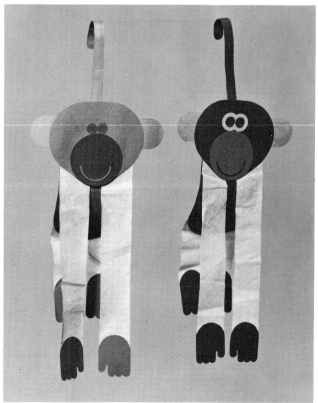

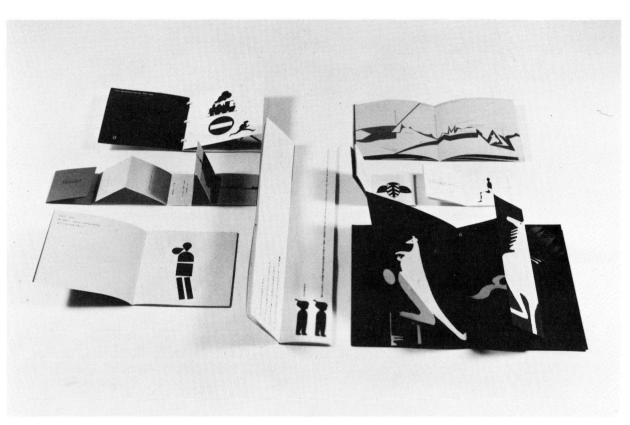

Graphic design is often influenced by painters and sculptors. The concept of space or form discovered by the artist becomes a part of the designer's visual vocabulary. Paul Klee has been a source of inspiration for many; Piet Mondrian's influence continually appears and reappears in contemporary design. Perhaps the greatest single influence on design was the teachers of the Bauhaus.

Of particular interest to designers working with three-dimensional forms is the work and teachings of Moholy Nagy. At this time in art history, explorations in light, motion, and film initiated in the twenties are being explored—explored dynamically, with the materials of our time, in the forms of our time. We, too, in the commercial world are employing the same techniques in our medium. Perhaps some of the fine art techniques have in turn been borrowed from commercial discoveries and technological achievements. Nevertheless, creative opportunities abound for the designer who is alert to them.

The following is presented as a brief respite in our journey.

Quite obviously, black and white photographs cannot portray the effects achieved by the various pieces illustrated. What is hoped is to alert the reader to these artists and their use of materials. Except for the Lippold structure, all the units depend on light and/or motion for their effects.

Julio Le Park, "Double Concurrence—Continuous Light, 2," (1961). A black wooden box 21 x 19¾ x 5⅝ inches with illuminated aperture 7⅞ x 8 inches, in which 54 plastic squares 1½ x 1½ inches, two reflectors, three sets of interchangeable pierced metal screens, and two glass filters interact. Collection, The Museum of Modern Art, New York. Philip Johnson Fund.

Thomas Wilfred, "Vertical Sequence Opus 137," detail, (1941). A lumia composition (projected light on ground glass screen). Form cycle seven minutes; color cycle 7 minutes 17 seconds; screen 15¼ x 15⅜ inches. Collection, The Musem of Modern Art, New York.

Richard Lippold, "Variation Number 7: Full Moon", (1949-50). Made of brass rods, nickel-chromium and stainless steel wire, it is ten feet tall. Collection, The Museum of Modern Art, New York. Mrs. Simon Guggenheim Fund.

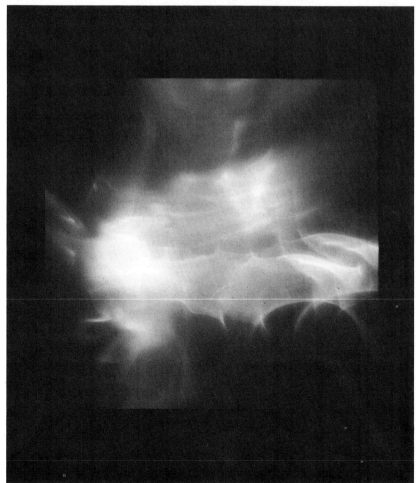

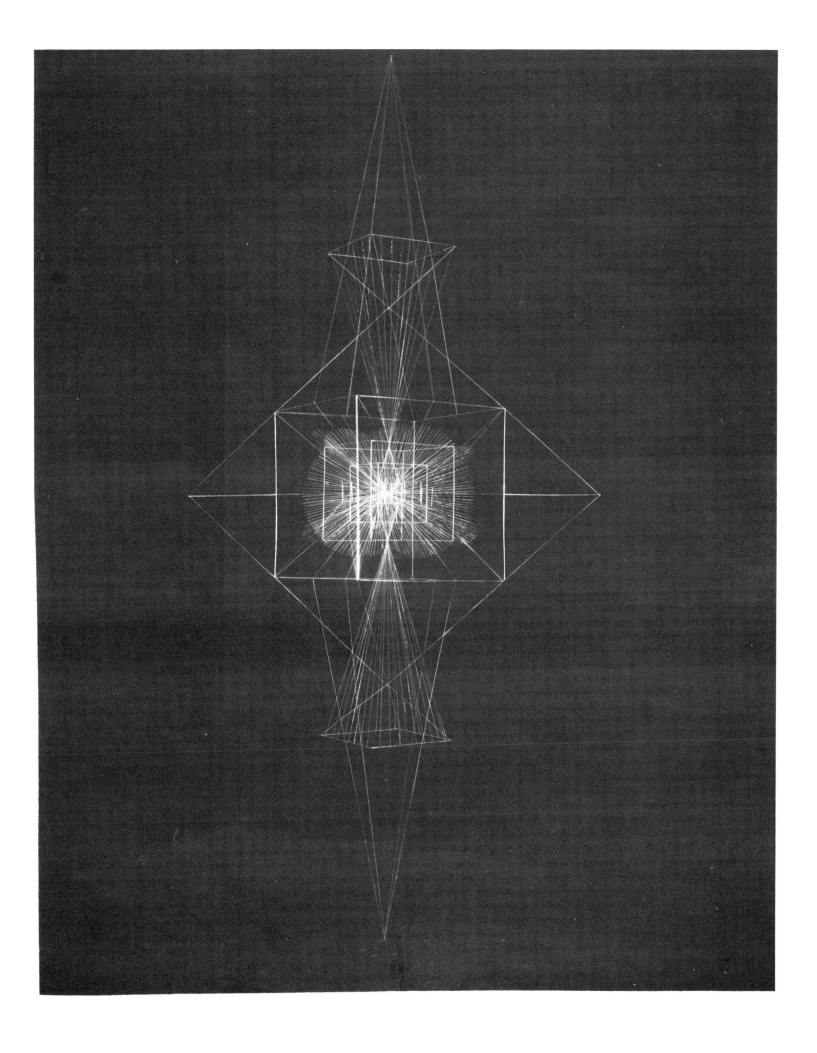

Nicolas Schoffer, "Microtemps II," (1965). A motorized construction of steel, duraluminum, and plexiglass, in a black wood box, 24⅛ x 34¼ inches. Collection, The Museum of Modern Art, New York. Frank Crowinshield Fund. The photograph below shows the unit in motion.

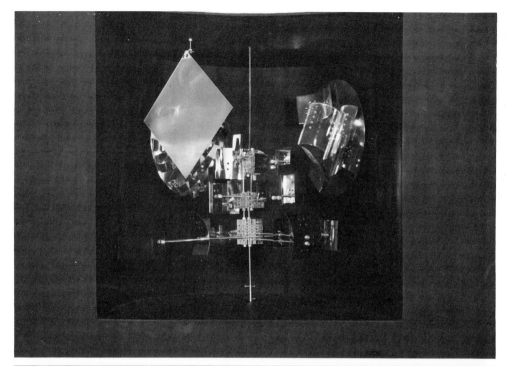

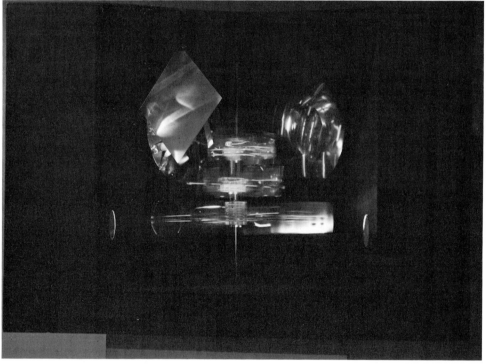

Chryssa, "Five Variations on the Amper-
sand," (1966). Five neon light constructions in tinted plexiglass vitrines; one is
30¼ x 14¼ x 12⅜ inches; four are
29½ x 14¼ x 12⅜ inches. Collection,
The Museum of Modern Art, New York.
Gift of Dominique and John de Menil.

Ronald Mallory. "Untitled," (1966). Motorized construction with mercury sealed
in plastic, 19¾ x 19¾ x 8 inches. The
inherent physical properties of mercury
make it collect into infinite forms as the
disc slowly rotates. Collection, The
Museum of Modern Art, New York. Larry
Aldrich Foundation Fund.

Eldorado Landi, "Geometrical Kinetic
Variations," (1963). Motorized construction of water-filled tubes, rollers with
colored cloth tape in a box, 19¾ x 19¾
x 5¾ inches. Collection, The Museum of
Modern Art, New York. Gift of the Olivetti
Company of Italy.

CONCLUSION

One of the most critical areas in the creation of point-of-purchase materials is scheduling. Effective administration and coordination in this area can avoid costly errors and delays. Properly administered and scheduled development is an ideal that, unfortunately, is not often achieved. Obviously there must be time for the development of the creative idea. Too often, the very first idea of the designer is quickly made into a working model in order to meet a schedule that is fictitious. This display will then sit in the client's office for a week or more. During this critical time, the designer could have had more time to be thinking along other lines and other means of expression. Instead, the display lies fallow on some desk because "it had to be there," when in reality it was never required at that time. And, often, this same unit will come back to be revised, restructured, reengineered — all working against a time schedule which should have been improved from the beginning.

The consequences of improper planning are reflected all along the line. In the manufacturing and production of a given unit, possibly the vacuum-form mold should be changed, but the manufacturer must make do because of insufficient time. The printer, who is conscious of quality control, may not have sufficient time to work his plates to ensure proper colors and fidelity.

How then can you determine a schedule so that there is not this chaos? What are the causes which must be corrected? To begin with, the salesman who says that his account wants a sketch overnight is negligent in his responsibility to his own design organization. He must remind the client that he is spending thousands of dollars on his promotion and that he cannot possibly expect it overnight. It is not fair to the advertiser or the manufacturer. What are the real deadlines? It is up to the salesman to make them known to you. This is also true for the advertiser. He is neglecting the needs of his own company if he delays in contacting his suppliers the moment he knows details of his promotion. Certainly, this industry is famous for being able to do the impossible in a very short time. But on a professional daily working level, the efficiency of an organization can be tremendously improved if the flow of materials through it can be properly timed.

We all can do rush jobs, but when every job has to be completed in a hurried atmosphere, the possibility of errors increases and the potential for creative thinking is diminished. Therefore, to whomever the responsibility falls, the correct scheduling and timing of point-of-purchase materials cannot be over emphasized.

What is the proper development time from a designer's point of view? Each of us is aware of how we perform best. We have had experiences where solutions arrive quickly because of pressure. We have also seen where time has helped the development and growth of an idea. How well we perform personally becomes a matter of our own professional capacities.

The proper amount of time also depends upon whether the designer is in a studio or with an advertiser or display manufacturer. The development of schedules within those organizations varies. The important thing for the designer to realize is that he bears a responsibility in the development of schedules. He must not permit his creative resources to be exploited and utilized as mere piece work. It is difficult to determine the work load an individual designer can perform. Obviously, the professional, if he is to survive, is often performing in excess of his own expectations. This is the nature of professionalism. It is abuse of our time because of the inefficient utilization of it that we must resist. We must make an effort to improve upon this situation. In the end, the primary function of the designer is to design.

Another problem of the point-of-purchase industry of major importance to the design community is what I call the "free-design syndrome." It has been with the industry from the start. The supposition of "free design" is that the advertiser does not pay for the design of the display submitted to him, but only for the manufacture of it. Nor does he pay for the design of rejected submissions.

The point-of-purchase manufacturers make up one of the most sophisticated and inventive industries in the world. In what other industry does a company custom-design, create tooling, assemble, produce, and mass-produce a product with hundreds of parts — all within six weeks? Display manufacturers, more often than not, have done the impossible; they have performed above and beyond even their wildest dreams. This is the excitement and challenge of point-of-purchase.

Unfortunately, this group of sophisticated business men, both manufacturers and their counterparts with the advertiser, fall prey to the wish for "something for nothing." Of all groups, of all industries, they should know that this is impossible. There isn't a display sold that doesn't have its costs plus profit included in the price. And rightly so. The display manufacturer calculates to the number of cuts, welds, and rivets the cost of a display. He must therefore charge for his design time, and this includes the cost of rejected submissions as well. It is acknowledged that the cost is hidden, charged in his overhead. The seller and buyer know this but, because of some unwritten code, no one admits it. Since the advertiser is in fact paying for design, he should be free to get the best design available for his money.

I question, therefore, how such an intelligent group of men can continue to perpetuate a myth about "free" design. Display manufacturer's designers are specialists in display design. On their abilities rests the success of every presentation made and every order sold. Offering its abilities free diminishes the pride and professionalism of the design staff and instills the seeds of complacency and mediocrity.

The buyers of this free design are equally guilty of misleading their companies. They buy a $100,000 promotion for their management, and they account for all the material costs and expenses. Everyone is pleased. And, added to that, they sell management "free" design. The company has a top advertising agency to handle its account. Millions of dollars are spent on creative answers to the company's advertising problems, to put the advertiser's visual image forward. To maintain that the display buyer can do it for nothing is deceiving management. It is selling them short — selling them short where they are most vulnerable — at the point of sale.

No company can afford to buy "free" design. It is an unreal myth that has resulted in much of the graphic clutter that has been associated with point-of-purchase. As long as the advertiser pays for it (and he does in one way or another), then let us in the industry divorce ourselves from this deception.

Among sophisticated advertisers, professional men trained in point-of-sale advertising are responsible for its development. But this is not always the case.

Point-of-sale material gets the leftover part of promotional dollars. Display requirements are nebulous; and they are often left in the hands of the purchasing department, with the instruction, "I have $35,000 left and I need a display." This requirement to "give us a display," in turn is passed on to three manufacturers. Each manufacturer devotes energy to creating a display on specula-

tion, in the hopes of getting the manufacturing order. While it is hoped that the manufacturer will know the merchandising requirements of the advertiser, this may not be so. His effort may revolve around submitting something he thinks the buyer may like, regardless of what is truly needed. Obviously, this is an extremely unprofessional way to spend money. All these individual promotions add up to huge annual expenditures by the advertiser.

In this manner, the advertiser is not getting value for his dollar. He is not getting a professional service geared to meet his specific needs. It is equivalent to his using a different advertising agency every time he does an ad. In addition, he is losing other services that should go hand-in-hand with each promotion. How effective was the display, where was it used, how was it received, how could it be improved? What did the salesmen, the store manager, the consumer think of it? Did it do the job? Was it in keeping with other corporate graphic material?

What can be done? For a start, a retainer could be given to a producer who offers professional marketing services. Rather than spend his creative energies on speculative and very different projects, this producer could concentrate his energies directly on the problems of his clients. With income assured, he can undertake to study fully the merchandising needs of his clients. He could develop a specialized staff that creates for these clients. With a fair determination of profit there should be no fear of excessive pricing on given units. Ideal, perhaps. Unrealistic, perhaps. Impractical to a degree, especially if the producer selected owns production facilities that he must keep running. This suggestion, certainly not original, is one way of bridging the gap that now exists in the industry.

The logical solution to these problems is the point-of-purchase agency devoting its services to specific clients, in the manner of advertising agencies. This point-of-purchase agency would be staffed with people familiar with the advertiser's specific marketing problem. It could then professionally solve display and related marketing problems. It would be oriented to both marketing and design, and would have the added responsibility of buying the displays for the advertisers. Certainly, one designer devoting his attention to the display problems of one account will be more effective knowing that what he does will be used. The advertisers, in turn, will know that the designer is concerned continually with their problems. The growth of these point-of-purchase agencies may well come out of the display houses now in existence.

It is not my intention to detail a solution. But it must be acknowledged that there is a need for a professional attitude about the point-of-purchase medium, so that its fullest potential may be explored. My concern is not with how this is arrived at, but with the necessity of achieving it.

The utilization of the point-of-purchase medium will become increasingly more important. The acceptance of this medium by advertiser management will aid in its growth. Management is coming to accept the value of point-of-purchase and its contribution to total marketing goals. Point-of-purchase is not just a "dump bin," but a vital sales tool. Companies are learning that the package on the development of which they spend countless hours and dollars requires an environment that the advertiser himself must request and develop.

In addition, advertising and manufacturing costs are high, and there must be substantial sales to offset them. There is too much time lag between sales messages and in-store buying. More dollars and attention therefore will have to be devoted to point-of-purchase. Whether it will come from television or print budgets depends on the nature of the advertiser. Possibly, point-of-purchase will receive more dollars without loss to other media. In any case, point-of-purchase will expand.

Therefore, the competition at the point of sale will be increased and the designer must be more creative in his solutions to problems. It won't help to redecorate last year's ideas. The development of new concepts of marketing, new concepts of display, new concepts of materials will be the challenge in point-of-purchase. The designer who studies the market place and looks for the new will be the creative leader of tomorrow.

GLOSSARY

ASSEMBLY. The process of erecting display component parts into a single, integrated display unit.

AUDIOVISUAL. A display using sound as well as sight to convey its advertising message. Also the hardware used for the purpose.

BACK-BAR DISPLAY. A display designed to be used behind the bar, or on the mirror behind the bar or fountain.

BACK CARD. A card unit attached to the back of a dump bin, floor bin or counter merchandiser which projects above the merchandise and presents the advertising message at eye level.

BAKED-ENAMEL SIGNS. Signs usually printed by the silk screen process on metal, employing synthetic resins, and baked at high temperatures to speed up the drying process and prolong the life of the sign.

BANNER. A piece of plastic, cloth or paper, usually in the form of a rectangle or triangle, suspended from its top in windows, from walls or overhead, or outdoors on ropes or wires between poles. Outdoor banners are usually printed on heavy canvas and have metal grommets for stays.

BIN. A holder for bulk merchandise. Can be made of wire, wood, corrugated, sheet metal, etc.

BLANK DUMMY. A mock-up full-size, serviceable model of a display with no printing or art.

BLEED. The part of the original art work which is carried beyond the illustration or background so that when the finished unit is cut or die-cut, no unprinted portion shows.

BLEED LOSS. That part of the bleed which is cut off.

BLISTER-PACK. A card containing an item covered with a transparent casing or cap attachment. Usually a non-food item or premium with a packaged food.

BOTTLE TOPPER. A small cardboard display designed to circle the neck of a bottle and carry an advertising message.

BROKER. A trader who purchases materials or commodities and resells them at a profit without making any alteration in the materials or commodities. Sometimes misapplied to point-of-purchase advertising agencies which design and sell but do not manufacture point-of-purchase materials.

CASH REGISTER DISPLAY. A display designed to be mounted on a cash register at a check-out spot in self-service stores. Usually designed to hold high impulse items such as candy, cigarettes, razor blades, etc. Also a sign, usually illuminated, mounted on the cash register on the bar or back bar.

CHANGE HOLDER. A rubber or plastic mat with a nubbly surface to keep coins from rolling off the counter when the clerk puts them down for the customer. Usually carries an advertising message.

COMPREHENSIVE (OR "COMP"). Finished or semi-finished piece of art—a drawing or model.

COPY. The printed advertising message.

COPY AREA. That part of a sign or display carrying the message.

COUNTER CARD. At the point of purchase, a card with brand name and product information designed for use on the checkout or service counter. It may be placed with the merchandise to serve as a reminder.

COUNTER DISPLAY. A small display designed to fit on an average store counter.

COUPON PAD. A deck or pack of coupons serrated or so taped for easy tear-off. Usually features a mail-in premium or a price rebate.

CROW'S FEET. A pair of metal brackets which fit into pole slots at right angles to each other and form feet for a pole display.

CUT-CASE. A shipping carton designed to be cut into shelf trays, each tray carrying product and a product message.

DEAL. An offer by an advertiser giving a free display, free merchandise, cash, or other considerations to the retailer for using the display, for buying a specified quantity of merchandise or performing other functions.

DEALER COPY. The space for the retailer to put his name, price, or other message on the advertiser's sign or display—also the copy he puts in.

DEALER INCENTIVE. A display having as an integral part some useful or desirable take-home unit for the dealer—tables, carts, grills, etc.

DEALER LOADER. See: DEALER INCENTIVE.

DEBOSSED SIGN. A sign in which all or part of the copy area is recessed or "pushed in" from the flat surface yet is an integral part of that surface.

DECAL. Short for decalcomania. A printed plastic or specially treated paper sign usually affixed to windows, doors, products or any smooth surface. May be of the water immersible or pressure-sensitive type.

DIE-CUT SIGN. A sign where the shape is altered or cut by other than straight lines in order to give configuration to the sign for purposes of design.

DIE-CUTTING. The process of cutting out special shapes by means of a die made for the purpose.

DISPENSER. A sign or display containing a literature pocket or a tear-off pad or a merchandising display containing a stock of merchandise for active selling.

DISPLAY. A device or an accumulation of devices which, in addition to identifying and/or advertising a company and/or product, may also merchandise, either by actually offering product for sale or by indicating its proximity. A display characteristically bears an intimate relationship with the product whereas a "sign" is more closely related to the name of the manufacturer, the retailer, or the product.

DISPLAY CARD. A piece of display advertising, printed or mounted on cardboard, for attachment to a display of merchandise.

DISPLAY CARTON. Carton designed to fold out into a display without removing the product.

DOUBLE-FACE. Corrugated board with both sides smooth. Any sign or display finished on two sides.

DUMMY. A mock-up of the finished sign or display. Can be rough or well-finished.

DUMMY MERCHANDISE. Empty packages, or bottles filled with colored water, etc., used instead of the live merchandise for purposes of display.

DUMP-BIN. A bin-shaped holder designed to stand on the floor containing merchandise in random order— so-called because the merchandise can be "dumped" in from the case.

EASEL. Free standing floor unit of wood, plastic or metal to support signs, large cards and frames, or a support attached to display card to enable it to stand.

EMBOSSED SIGN. A sign on which all or part of the copy area is raised so that it stands out from the flat surface, yet is an integral part of that surface.

EMBOSSING. Process of raising prints, designs, patterns, etc., so that they are raised above the flat surface or signs or displays.

END-AISLE DISPLAY. A display particularly built for placement at the end of a store aisle which accommodates a large group of product units.

END DISPLAYS. Mass displays stacked against the end of a gondola or tier of groceries.

EXPOSED MERCHANDISE. Merchandise kept in sight of consumers on shelves and counters, readily accessible to clerks or customers.

EXTRUDED ALUMINUM. A finished piece of aluminum which has been produced by conforming it to shape by passing it through the die.

FACINGS. The number of packages of an item on the front line of the store shelf.

FEET. Various styles of display stands made of wire or corrugated board.

FLANGE SIGN. A sign made so that it can be mounted vertically to the surface of a wall, building or post, from which it projects. It has "Sell" copy on both sides.

FLASHER. A light that flashes on and off at timed intervals to attract attention.

FLOCKING. An electrostatic spraying process producing a velvety finish on any surface.

FLUORESCENT INK. An ink with high light-reflecting properties, hence attention-getting.

FOUR-COLOR PROCESS. See: PROCESS COLOR.

FREQUENCY. In point-of-purchase exposure, the number of times an individual sign or display is exposed to individuals within a specified time period.

GIANT REPLICA. An over-sized reproduction of the product or the trade mark.

GONDOLA. Island shelving, open on two sides, common to self-service stores.

GONDOLA END. A display designed to be used at the end of a gondola (set of

shelves) in a self-service store. "Gondola Ends" are usually large displays.

GONDOLA TOPPER. A two-sided display designed to rest on the top of the gondola in such a way that it can be seen from both aisles, or coming and going in both aisles.

GRAVITY FEED. A merchandiser designed to use the force of gravity to bring more merchandise into view as that already on view is sold. This can feed a single unit or a quantity in succession.

GRIPPER EDGE. The area along the edges of a printing sheet which gives allowance for mechanical fingers to pick up the sheet and carry it through the printing or die cutting press.

HANGING SIGN. A sign which hangs from a mounting bracket that usually projects from a wall, building, or post. It usually features copy on both sides.

HARDBOARD. A fabricated board material often used in displays.

HEADER. A message board projecting above the display and giving the headline or the advertising message. Usually larger or more intricate than a riser.

HEAT MOTOR. A small rotating element which is operated by the heat of an inside light. May be used to give the illusion of such effects as falling water, blowing drapery, etc., in a display.

IDENTIFICATION SIGN. A sign furnished by the advertiser and in addition to the advertising message bearing the firm name of the retailer, bank, etc. Also a sign giving the firm name only in a place of business.

IMPULSE ITEMS. Those products which have a high appeal to the consumer and cause her to make an unplanned purchase. Items are described as "high" or "low" impulse.

INFLATABLE. A plastic creation which assumes three dimensions when filled with air or gas. May be used as a premium or an integral part of the display.

IN-PACK. A premium packed inside a product package as an incentive for consumer purchase.

INJECTION-MOLDING. The process of shaping plastic pieces inside a mold.

INSERT. An advertisement package with retail merchandise.

INSTALLATION SERVICE. Service offered by a company which contracts to place displays in retail outlets for the advertiser at so much per unit.

INSTRUCTION SHEET. Printed instructions giving directions for setting up a display.

ISLAND. A display designed to stand along with merchandise available from all sides.

LAMINATING. A process which consists of spreading a clear, bright, thin coat of plastic over a printed surface, giving a high degree of brilliance and protects the surface against wear.

LENTICULAR. A grooved plastic sheet with certain light properties which give a different visual angle at different light angles, creating a three dimensional effect when either printed or reprinted.

LETTERPRESS. Oldest method of mechanical printing in which printing ink is transferred from raised metal to paper, board, etc.

LINKAGE. Connections from the motor to the moving parts of a motion display. This can be more or less complicated depending upon the type of motion wanted.

LOCKS. On cardboard displays tabs that secure display sections or pieces in the intended position.

LOGO. The advertiser's stylized trade name or trademark to be used repeatedly in his advertising.

MASS DISPLAY. A display featuring a sizeable grouping of the product plus the message.

MERCHANDISER. A display containing merchandise for immediate sale.

MINIATURE. A small scale model of a large and/or expensive display. Also, a small sketch very much underscale and usually rough.

MOBILE. A display consisting of several counter-balanced pieces suspended in such a way that each piece moves independently in a light current of air.

MOCK UP. Facsimile sample of point-of-purchase signs and displays indicative of proposed production unit.

MODULAR DISPLAYS. Erector set system, permitting the building of a variety of displays from a few basic units.

MOLDS. Patterns or forms from which metal or plastic sign and display elements are produced.

MOTION DISPLAYS. Any signs or displays with moving elements to attract attention.

MOUNTING AND FINISHING. Bonding the printed sheet to reinforcement, die-cutting, scoring, etc. Joining parts in sub-assembly or assembly.

OFF-PACK. A display containing product and premiums, or just premiums, but in either case they are physically connected to each other.

OFFSET PRINTING. A process in which impressions are transferred from the engraving plate to a rubber blanket and then printed on paper.

ON-PACK. A premium fastened to the outside of the merchandise package to give appeal and attention value to the product as against its competitors.

OVERRUN. Additional copies of printed material beyond the number ordered. This is necessary whenever more than one operation is required to produce the final product. The printer must speculate on how many pieces will be required to offset accidental damage in each intervening process so that he may come out with at least the number ordered.

OVER-THE-WIRE BANNER. A long rectangular piece of paper with the product message printed twice (head to head) on one side of the paper. When thrown over a wire, the messages are back to back and can be seen from either side. These are also used over T-bars. Frequently, a series of smaller banners over one wire.

P-O-P. Common abbreviation for point-of-purchase advertising.

P-O-P ADVERTISING AGENCY. A creator, programmer and supplier of point-of-purchase advertising materials who operates without manufacturing facilities, but with creative facilities geared to client needs.

P-O-P PRODUCER/SUPPLIER/MANUFACTURER. A supplier of point-of-purchase advertising materials who may or may not own production facilities as well as creative facilities for supplying point-of-purchase materials.

P-O-S. Point-of-Sale advertising—used interchangeably with P-O-P.

PENCIL ROUGH. Drawing of the proposed sign or display usually in the preliminary stages and in a loose style. Term implies a rough sketch rendered with any implement.

PERMANENT DISPLAY. A display designed for use for an indefinite length of time.

PERSONALIZED DISPLAY. A display with retailer's name, etc., to make it exclusive for him.

PHOTOGELATINE. A direct, screenless printing process which reproduces continuous tones with maximum fidelity. It allows facsimile reproduction on any original copy; in fact, any type of art work, monotone or multi-color. This method is used for printing point-of-purchase transparencies and posters on paper and vinyl. The printing plate in this process consists of a thin film of chemically treated gelatine, which has been spread over a special metal plate.

POINT-OF-PURCHASE ADVERTISING. Selling the product or brand name story to customers of a retail outlet at that outlet.

POINT-OF-PURCHASE ADVERTISING MATERIALS. Those devices or structures located in, on, or at the retail outlet which identify, advertiser, and/or merchandise the outlet, a service, or a product, as an aid to retail selling.

POLE. Round cardboard tube to hold display above a stack of merchandise, usually in several sections. Also a metal pole on which display or sign is erected.

POLE DISPLAY. A display mounted on a footed pole designed to be used with massed merchandise, and to be seen above it. The pole is mostly hidden in use.

POLE SIGN. Single or double-faced, attached to poles at gasoline stations, and other outlets.

POLE TOPPER. The display part of the pole display.

POPAI. The Point-of-Purchase Advertising Institute, Inc., the trade association representing the P-O-P industry.

PORCELAIN SIGNS. Signs of porcelain on metal, usually printed by the silk screen process, each color being applied and fused separately onto the metal. Extremely durable and long-lived, they are used extensively by companies whose advertising approach remains constant for extended periods of time.

POSTER. A printed plastic, paper or cloth banner or sign for window or interior use.

PRE-PACK. A display designed to be packed with merchandise by the advertiser and shipped as a unit.

PRESSURE-SENSITIVE. A common adhesive material usually available in strips or solid coverage used to adhere signs, etc., to posting position desired.

PRIVILEGE COPY/PANEL AREA. Part of display for private or exclusive use of retailer.

PROCESS COLOR. Inks of four colors—yellow, magenta, intense blue and black—which when printed in sequence, one over the other, give the effect of natural color. Also known as "Four-Color Process."

PROMOTIONAL DISPLAY. In the broad sense, all displays are "promotional," but the word "promotional" is also used to indicate a display which is designed to be used only for the duration of a particular promotion, as opposed to those pieces which are designed for use for an indefinite period (See: PERMANENT DISPLAY and SEMI-PERMANENT DISPLAY).

PUBLIC SERVICE DISPLAY. Display containing a clock, thermometer, baseball scores, etc., of interest to customers but not necessarily related to the product.

PUMP TOPPER. Display used on top of gasoline pumps.

RACK. A floor stand featuring shelves, pockets or hooked arms, usually of wire, designed for special display of a group of related items—sometimes a sub-department—for customer self-service and/or self-selection. Racks may or may not also carry an advertiser message.

READER. See: RISER.

REDEMPTION COUPON. A coupon which, when mailed to the advertiser or presented to the dealer, entitles the consumer to acquire the advertised product at a discount or without charge.

RISER. That part of a display which projects above the merchandising presentation—or a sign or display which rises from the top shelf of an aisle or is placed atop a pole and so is visible from other parts of the store.

RUBBER-PLATE PRINTING. The process of reproducing from rubber plates, usually on combined corrugated board, eliminating the need of printing on lithograph sheets and then mounting to corrugated.

SCORING. A partial cut through cardboard or crease impression to allow for bending of board.

SELF SELECTOR. A display containing merchandise organized in such a way that the customer may readily select color, size, style, etc.

SEMI-PERMANENT DISPLAY. A display sturdy enough to be used for a seasonal promotion, such as Christmas or spring, but not intended for indefinite use. It would customarily outlast several short-term promotions and would serve as the encompassing carrier of a seasonal theme.

SHELF-EXTENDER. A display in the form of a small tray, designed to be fastened or clamped to a shelf and to project from it, to extend the space of the shelf. It is usually used for related item sales.

SHELF-MISER. A small display designed to fit on the shelf and to hold more units in the same space than would ordinarily be on the shelf. These frequently have a spring or gravity-feed arrangement to keep the front of the facing full.

SHELF TALKER. A printed card designed to lay on the shelf under the product and project out and down to carry an advertising message which will call attention to the product. The flap end is frequently die-cut. It is sometimes held in place with pressure-sensitive adhesive.

SIGN. Any device which identifies a company or a product and/or carries an advertising or directional message. Signs may be separate entities, or an integral part of a display. "Signs" as commonly used means separate entities.

SILK-SCREEN PROCESS. A method of printing one color at a time through a stencil securely affixed to a porous surface on a screen of silk. The color used in this process is a paste, which, when pushed through the pores of the silk, leaves an even coating on stock placed under the screen. All parts of the design not to be printed have been rejected by an impermeable substance.

STITCHING, Fastening of parts of displays to each other or to holders with heavy wire staples.

STREAMER. See: POSTER.

SUPPLIER. Advertiser's source of P-O-P materials. Usually the manufacturer of the display material.

TAB. A small flap fastened to the edge of displays, sometimes conveying an extra advertising message or reminder. Also the part inserted into a slot to fasten parts of a display.

TACKER SIGN. A sign made so that it can be tacked or nailed to a building, a fence, etc. It has copy on one side only.

TAG STOCK. A thin flexible cardboard.

TAKE-ONE PAD. A pad for customer tear-off used as part of a sign or display.

TESTER. Unit designed with actual merchandise that consumer is encouraged to test.

TIE-IN. Cooperative advertising effort between multiple products featured together in one display unit, usually at a money-saving combination price, e.g., toothbrush—toothpaste, razor—shaving cream—after shave lotion. Products are sometimes manufactured by different companies.

TOOLING. The process of readying productive facilities for mass production of point-of-purchase materials. Also spoken of as "tooling up."

UNDERRUN. The number of displays or printed material short of the number specified in the order. See also: OVERRUN.

VACUUM-FORMING. An inexpensive process by which light service plastic signs and displays are shaped to three-dimensional figures by use of vacuum machinery.

WINDOW DISPLAY. A retail outlet display placed in the windows facing outside to attract the attention of pedestrians passing the establishment.

WINDOW STREAMER. A long narrow advertisement attached to a store window.

WOOD GRAIN. Application of a wood-like finish to metal, paper and other materials other than wood.

The author wishes to thank the Point of Purchase Advertising Institute for the use of this glossary, which was developed by them.

CREDITS